ENCYCLOPEDIA OF ESTATE PLANNING

ENCYCLOPEDIA OF

ESTATE PLANNING

ROBERT S. HOLZMAN

BOARDROOM® CLASSICS

55 Railroad Avenue, Greenwich, CT 06830

Completely Revised Edition
10 9 8 7 6 5 4 3 2 1

Library of Congress Cataloging in Publication Data

Holzman, Robert S.
   Encyclopedia of estate planning

   Includes index.
   1. Estate planning—United States.
I. Title.
KF750.Z9H65 1985B   346.7305'2   86-31031
ISBN 0-88723-126-8   347.30652

Boardroom® Classics is a registered trademark of Boardroom,® Inc.
55 Railroad Ave., Greenwich, CT 06830

Printed in the United States of America

Table of Contents

Chapter One

LEAVE NOTHING TO CHANCE— MAKE A WILL

Your will is a statement directing the disposition of your property when you die. Not only does a will ensure that your assets go to recipients of your choice, it also specifies how and when they are to receive them. If, for example, a beneficiary is young or financially unsophisticated, the will might provide that the property go to a trustee or a guardian for a specified period of time, with the income of the trust being assigned to the beneficiary.

If you die without leaving a valid will, however, the disposition of your property will be in accordance with the intestacy laws of the state in which you reside. The property will go to your next of kin in proportions and in a sequence mandated by the state. If there is no will, and there is no known next of kin within the definition of state law, your property may revert to the state.

What the will should do

Most important, the will should name the executor who will administer your estate. This means locating all assets, pursuing claims and collecting what is due, disposing of assets in the most favorable manner possible, and following specific instructions or exercising such discretion as you have decided on. To ensure that your estate is managed by those of ability, interest, and loyalty, you should name contingent or successor executors.

Further, if you die without leaving a valid will, or if the executor you named is unable or unwilling to serve, a state court will choose for your estate an administrator who is paid out of its assets. He/she may be interested only in collecting a fee, which could be far greater than the services he/she renders are worth. (See Chapter Forty-six, "Avoiding Appointment of an Administrator.")

After you have selected a reliable executor and successor executor, don't let the matter rest there. If, over the years, they become unable or unwilling to serve, adjust your will and name new executors. And if you have minor children, the will should certainly name a guardian for them. Your choice of guardian might be the most important asset you can provide for them.

Your words and intentions may have to be interpreted

Bear in mind the fact that your will is a legal document. It should be prepared by a lawyer—but not just any lawyer will do. Law, like medicine, is highly specialized. The attorney who handles your business affairs may be competent in matters concerning contracts, claims, and other commercial matters, but unless he/she has specialized knowledge in the field of estate planning, various traps are likely to be overlooked. There are standards that must be met if the will is to serve your purposes. In commenting on one suit where a decedent's will had been prepared by his brother-in-law, who was an insurance agent and not an attorney, the court observed sadly, "This tax litigation is the consequence." Do not make the mistake of thinking that any written attempt to pass on property will create the desired dispositions.

Be certain that the will expresses what you have in mind without ambiguity. Beneficiaries should be identified by name—"my son" means little if another boy is born after the will was drawn. Review the will when children are born, marry, or die, and when Congress enacts substantial changes in the tax law.

The will should provide for contingent beneficiaries if a named beneficiary dies before you do, or if the beneficiary, for whatever reason, refuses the bequest. This precaution prevents assets from being dissipated by being divided many times among next of kin or even lost outright through escheat, or reversion to the state.

What a will cannot do

Even with a well-drawn will you do not, in fact, have full discretion as to the disposition of your property. State law dictates varying percentages of the estate that a surviving spouse is entitled to receive. The state in which you are domiciled may require that a surviving wife receive 35 percent of your property as dower; if you leave her a lesser amount, she can "take against the will," receiving her 35 percent at the expense of your other beneficiaries. The corresponding right that may be claimed by a surviving husband is called curtesy. In some states, children are entitled to specified percentages of the estate regardless of whether the parent made provision for them in his/her will.

A decedent's right to dispose of property is still further limited in a few states—for example, state law may hold that bequests to charitable organizations are not valid unless made more than 30 days before death.

A will may not carry out a testator's wishes if he/she hasn't anticipated various problems. It may not be possible on the basis of existing records for the executor to prove that the decedent had clear title to, or full ownership of, the property he/she wished to convey. The executor may not be able to identify or locate certain assets. Or the will makes certain bequests, but the estate lacks the money or property to implement them.

Conclusions and advice

- Make certain that your executor will know where your assets are and what your exact intentions are.

- Have your will reviewed when there are changes in the tax law, in the needs of your beneficiaries, in your income and theirs. If you move to a different state, check to see whether formal requirements are different, such as the minimum number of witnesses required.

- Do not assume that you can leave your property to anyone you select, in whatever amounts you see fit.

- Do not assume that once you have made a will, everything will be taken care of according to your directions.

- Do not assume that your excellent family or business lawyer will also be competent in the entirely different field of estate planning.

4

Chapter Two

HIDDEN TRAPS IN ESTATE PLANNING

The objective of estate planning—the transmission of as much of one's wealth as possible to chosen parties in the most appropriate manner—requires the avoidance of many traps and pitfalls. Otherwise, unnecessary taxes and other forms of diminution will erode what goes to the beneficiaries, and one's intentions may be frustrated substantially—or even entirely.

Major traps

Proper planning can anticipate the traps lurking in these principal areas:

1. Retention of some form of control over property so that it is deemed to be part of the transferor's gross estate when he/she dies, even though he/she has parted with the assets and is not exercising any control over them. (See Chapter Forty-three, "The Dry Run.") Avoidance of strings may have to be part of one's planning. For example, a father may have

transferred assets to a trust for the benefit of his minor children, reserving the right to allocate trust property to each child until the youngest reached age 21, by which time the father felt that he would know enough about the financial and other strengths of each child to make a final decision. But before that date arrived, the father became mentally incompetent. He could not release the retained power, and inevitably the property was taxed as part of his estate when he died. No one could do anything about it.

2. The making of gifts or other transfers in good faith, and in compliance with state laws. For example, transfers of real estate, to be valid under state law, may have to be in writing. In some states the transfer is not effective until it is recorded in a designated county office.

3. The holding of property in joint ownership. This can be disastrous if the parties become estranged and hostile. In addition, the Internal Revenue Service includes half the value of the property in the gross estate of the first co-owner to die if the co-owners are husband and wife.

Unless the executor can prove otherwise, the IRS will include the *full* value of the property in the estate of the first co-owner to die, except in the case of the jointly held residence of a married couple under certain circumstances. (See Chapter Eighteen, "Choice of Forms of Ownership.")

4. Unwitting possession of incidents of ownership of insurance on the decedent's life. A young man may take out insurance on his life, naming his mother as beneficiary. The salesman might think that when his client gets married, he will want to change the name of the beneficiary, so the policy reserves the right to make the change to the insured. After marriage, he gives the policy to his bride. But since he has the right to change the name of the beneficiary, even after his wife has been desig-

nated, the proceeds will be includable in his gross estate when he dies.

5. Reliance upon the wrong "experts." The seller of an insurance policy may claim that the transaction can be arranged so that the proceeds will be exempt from federal estate tax. That statement isn't good enough for the Internal Revenue Service and the courts. Or an insurance agent, as part of an estate plan, may recommend to his/her client that certain policies or contracts be exchanged for others. True, some policies may be exchanged on a tax-free basis. But not all types of insurance, endowment, or annuity contracts may be exchanged tax-free. A tax specialist should check the Internal Revenue Code requirements in order to ascertain whether ordinary income tax is payable upon the exchange.

6. Failure of an attorney to follow instructions. One woman told her son, a practicing lawyer, that she wanted to make a gift to her six children, to be apportioned equally. She gave him a substantial sum and told him to invest the money in a mutual fund in such a way as to set up trust funds for the children, since she didn't need the money. Fearful that his mother would not have sufficient income, he deviated from her instructions and had the mutual-fund company draw up a trust in which his mother would retain the right to take trust income and principal if she needed funds, the remaining principal to be apportioned among the surviving children when she died. She learned of his deviation only when she began getting money from the trustee, which at its own discretion sent her checks. She ordered her son to conform to her original intention that the trust be irrevocable with no reservation to herself. But he had not done this by the time she died, so the principal was included in her gross estate—even though she had no intention of retaining any strings on her gift.

7. Reliance upon the IRS. If the testator, his/her executor, or attorney asks the IRS about the tax treatment of an item and the reply is faithfully followed, tax and interest will still be imposed if this advice was incorrect. In the words of a famous judge, "Harsh as it may be, one accepts the advice of a revenue official at his peril." But under the so-called Taxpayer Bill of Rights of 1988, there will be no penalty where a taxpayer *can show* that he/she had relied upon *written* information furnished by Internal Revenue Service personnel acting in their official capacity.

The Revenue Reconciliation Act of 1989 expanded the list of authorities upon which taxpayers may rely (previously contained in Treasury regulations) to include proposed regulations, private letter rulings, technical advice memoranda, actions on decisions, general counsel memoranda, information or press releases, notices, and any other similar documents published by the IRS in the *Internal Revenue Bulletin* and the General Explanation of tax legislation prepared by the Joint Committee on Taxation. The IRS is required to publish not less frequently than annually a list of positions for which the service believes there is no substantial authority and which affect a significant number of taxpayers.

8. An inexperienced executor or executrix. Errors and omissions made by the fiduciary can be very costly to the estate and to the beneficiaries, although, under certain circumstances, it is the executor who is held personally liable for his/her mistakes. Frequently, for sentimental reasons or as a gesture of confidence, a husband names his wife or adult child to serve as executor or executrix. This could be a very bad mistake, both from the points of view of the estate and of the fiduciary, who may have to make good from his own pocket. A person may seek to save an inexperienced

relative from the consequences of his/her unfamiliarity with the subject by providing in the will that the executor won't be required to make good for his/her failure to exercise reasonable care, diligence, and prudence. Some state laws, however, hold that such a provision in a will is void.

9. The terms of a will may be contradictory, hampering at least some of the testator's wishes. For example, the marital deduction is available only where property passes to the surviving spouse. But not infrequently a will contains a basic contradiction providing (a) that all remaining property will go to the surviving spouse, and (b) that any property remaining after her death will go to the children or other designated parties. The marital deduction may be lost because the property did not go to the surviving spouse either outright or as qualified terminable interest property. Even if (a) states that the property is to go to her outright, in fee simple, (b) could contradict that.

10. An estate plan may have been devised solely on the basis of tax considerations. Taxes are an important element of estate planning, probably the single most important element. But they should not be the only matter considered. For example, in order to qualify for the maximum marital deduction, a husband may leave his entire estate, or a very substantial part of it, to his surviving spouse. She may have no need—or desire—for more wealth. But because of this tax motivation, little or nothing is available for his sister, or his children by a first marriage, or other persons he would like to see provided for.

11. A decedent's instructions or acts may result in excessive estate-tax valuations. One individual left instructions to his executor to retain a certain stock despite its ups and downs in the stock market. The IRS claimed that these shares should be valued at more than the market price,

asserting that the decedent had probably known more about the company than anyone else, and hence his estimate of its worth was more reliable than that of outsiders. Sometimes a person will list his residence for sale with a broker so that he can deduct insurance and maintenance charges as being in connection with property held primary for sale. Actually, he doesn't really want or intend to sell but only to claim some deductions, so he lists the house at such a high figure that there will be no buyers. The IRS is apt to value the house at the inflated figure that he himself had set to discourage buyers.

12. Use of unqualified appraiser. A competent appraiser can save considerably on estate taxes; an incompetent one is a liability. In one case, the values set by the executor's appraiser were far lower than those set by the IRS's appraisers. The court accepted the latter because cross-examination revealed that the executor's appraiser had once failed the American Institute of Real Estate Appraiser's examination.

13. Despite their advantages, buy-sell agreements can contain many traps. (See Chapter Twenty-two, "Buy-Sell Agreements.") If a shareholder owns enough stock to name a corporation's president and directors, it is dangerous for the corporation to carry insurance on his/her life to fund such an agreement. Here the proceeds would be includable in his/her gross estate. (See Chapter Twenty-five, "Planning with Life Insurance.") Implementation of a buy-sell plan may concentrate stock ownership of a corporation with nonoperating income in so few hands that undistributed income will be subject to a 28 percent personal-holding-company tax. In a buy-sell agreement, beware of a formula clause so complicated that the survivor of a deceased shareholder can demand an accounting or otherwise

put the corporation to great trouble.

14. Acceptance of a general power of appointment can be very costly. (See Chapter Thirty-six, "Powers of Appointment.") Often the existence of such a power isn't recognized by the parties. When he was 10 years old, one individual's parents set up a trust for his benefit to last 21 years. At any time, he or his legally appointed guardian could terminate the trust or withdraw any of its principal or accumulated income. Although not so labeled, this amounted to a general power of appointment. So when this person died at age 28, the value of the trust property was included in his gross estate. The fact that he never knew he had a general power of appointment, which could have been exercised or nullified before his death, was irrelevant.

15. Throwing out records relevant to the establishment of tax liability. Destruction of records (by the decedent's wife, for example, when she wants to straighten out the house) can result in higher taxes because proper claims and deductions on income- and estate-tax returns can't be substantiated. Incidentally, an individual who prematurely destroys evidence needed in a tax audit is subject to personal penalties. (See Chapter Forty-four, "A Letter to Your Executor.")

16. Gifts of income-producing properties to young children (under 14) may no longer save federal taxes. A child's unearned income in excess of $1,200 is taxed at the parents' top marginal rates. The child's minimum tax liability cannot exceed the amount by which the parents' minimum tax liability would be increased if the parents' tentative minimum and regular tax were increased by the amount of the child's tentative minimum tax and regular tax.

17. Beneficiaries who become nonbeneficiaries because of death prior

to the testator's or refusal to accept what had been left to them. Provide for contingent beneficiaries so that your property will go to persons of your own choice even though it may be a second choice.

18. Waiting too long. Gifts not made on an annual basis can mean loss of annual gift-tax exclusions. (See Chapter Nine, "Taking Advantage of the Annual Exclusion.") Transfers within three years of death can remove the property from the gross estate; but the former presumption still applies to transactions such as the release of retained power. And if an individual waits too long to take out additional life insurance to implement an estate plan, he/she may have become uninsurable.

19. Inflation can make your planned disposition unrealistic. (See Chapter Forty-one; Chapter Thirty; Chapter Twenty-six.)

20. The greatest trap of all is complacency, the belief that all of the pieces will automatically and satisfactorily fall into place.

Conclusions and advice

• The value of property transferred to other persons within three years of a decedent's death is no longer includable in that person's gross estate except in these areas: where the decedent had transferred insurance on his/her life to another person but had retained significant incidents of ownership (such as the right to change the name of the beneficiary); where the decedent had transferred property but the transfer was incomplete, such as where he/she had retained life estate or still had the right to alter, amend, or terminate the arrangement; or where he/she had some other continuing interest in the property. With certain exceptions, a grantor-retained interest in a trust does not remove the property from his/her estate.

Chapter Three

THE TRUST AS FINANCIAL UMBRELLA

One of the primary functions of an estate plan is to give the estate owner peace of mind. A successful estate plan can ensure that one's wealth or its income will be safeguarded against inexperience, diminishing abilities in advancing years, or the impact of unpredictable events. A trust is one of the most effective vehicles for establishing this peace of mind.

The trust is a separate and distinct entity from its creator. A trust holds property and performs acts in its own name for the benefit of one or more other parties. The creator of a trust abandons dominion over property to the trust. If he/she fails to abandon his incidents of control over the trust sufficiently, the trust won't serve to insulate him from ownership of its property or income. That is, he will not be insulated from estate and income taxation. If a trust is properly set up and operated, what had been a person's property or its income will be used to carry out his wishes, but he is protected from the tax and certain other consequences of property ownership. It is only retention of powers over the trust or its properties that determines taxability.

The person who forms a trust is known as the grantor, the trustor, or the settlor, among other names. The trust itself is created under the law of a particular state, and this can provide the opportunity for some shopping around. The laws of some states, for example, allow greater freedom for the investment of trust assets, such as in common stock.

The trustee is named to administer the property and to distribute it to the beneficiaries in accordance with the directions of the grantor. Neither the grantor nor the spouse should serve as a trustee of the trust, unless the powers of the trustee are purely administrative and permit no exercise of discretion.

• A trust created by a decedent's will is a testamentary trust; a trust created by an individual while alive is an inter vivos trust.

• If the grantor is able to terminate the trust, it is revocable; otherwise it is irrevocable.

• If all of the trust's income must be distributed each year to named beneficiaries, with no discretion lodged in the trustee, it is a simple trust; otherwise it is a complex trust.

Uses of trusts in estate planning

Here are some widely used forms of estate plans involving the use of trusts:

1. An individual wants to give property to persons too young or too financially unsophisticated to own property. The property can be

transferred to a trust with a knowledgeable trustee who will safeguard the principal and provide the beneficiaries with the income to the extent called for in the trust agreement. Variations on this plan can be used to turn the principal over to the beneficiaries under certain conditions, if this is desired, or to increase payments to beneficiaries when there are special needs for money.

2. An individual wishes to transfer property to relatives or other people or organizations without actually giving them the property at this time. By transferring the property irrevocably to a trust, he has gotten the value of this property out of what will be his gross estate when he dies. Death within three years of setting up the trust will trigger inclusion only if the grantor has retained powers in himself, or his death triggers distributions under the trust. Meanwhile, the property will be held by the trust, the trustee having been given powers to determine who will eventually get the property or certain proportions of it. For example, the trustee (but not the grantor) may be given discretion to transfer property or income to named persons or classes of people (such as the grantor's children or grandchildren, unidentified by name) according to their personal needs or business objectives.

3. A person may have greater income than he needs. Interest, dividends, rents, and the like from income-producing properties are being taxed at his maximum tax rate because of his high business earnings. He can transfer whatever portion of these income-producing properties he chooses to a trust for the benefit of relatives, friends, or charitable organizations for any period longer than 10 years. During this period the beneficiaries, not the grantor, will be taxed on the income (charitable organizations escape this). At

a later date—perhaps 15 years later—selected when the trust was created, the trust will terminate. It might have been thought that a limited life trust would be appropriate; for by the end of that period of time, the income beneficiaries will have established their own substantial earnings pattern or will have been relieved of the financial burden of raising children. When the trust is terminated, the remaining principal may go to any other party that was designated when the trust was created, except the grantor or his/her spouse. The grantor or spouse may get back the property only upon the death of the income beneficiary who is a lineal descendant of the grantor. (See Chapter Four, "The Short-Term Trust.")

4. A father may wish to give property to his son but fears that the beneficiary's gambling or other extravagances will result in the property ending up in the hands of his creditors. (See Chapter Six, "Spendthrift Trusts.")

5. An individual agrees to transfer property for the benefit of someone else but wishes to get this property back again under certain circumstances. For example, the use of an alimony trust permits an ex-husband to transfer property for the benefit of his former wife, but upon her death or remarriage, her right to the use of the income from this property will cease and another party—not the grantor or his subsequent spouse—will become the beneficiary. The trust agreement should designate the contingent party, which might, typically, be a named hospital or university.

6. An individual may wish to make permanent provision for the care of a handicapped child. He transfers income-producing property to a trust to provide for the lifetime maintenance and comfort of the child. The child

is assured of care despite the father's possible business reverses.

7. An individual wants to make certain that his business will be operated after his death for the benefit of his family. Left to his own devices, his executor, if not familiar with business problems and if anxious to be rid of his responsibilities as quickly as possible, would probably sell the enterprise as soon as he/she can, very likely for an inadequate price. To prevent this, a testamentary trust can be set up so that the trustees chosen for their commercial experience and reliability will continue the business instead of disposing of it. (See Chapter Twenty-four, "Business-Continuation Arrangements.")

8. A husband would like to provide a suitable annual income for his wife for as long as she lives. She doesn't want the problems of administering properties. He sets up a trust to which he supplies income-producing assets that will provide the desired amount, with the principal to go to named charities when she dies. But he is concerned that this income may prove to be insufficient because of extraordinary medical expenses or the failure of other investments he has given her. So the trustee is given the right to use the principal for the wife's benefit under certain defined circumstances.

9. A person has named several beneficiaries in his will, but much of his property is in a form that can't satisfactorily be divided into a number of parts: a business block, a collection of first editions, a producing oil well, a partnership in a fast-food franchise. Fractional interests, if they could be sold at all, would bring a much lower price. Beneficiaries will predictably have different ideas as to the time to sell and the price to ask. So the property owner transfers his properties to a trust, and the beneficiaries

receive fractional interests in the trust. The trustee, in his sole discretion, will sell the entire property as a unit at the proper time and price for the benefit of all the beneficiaries.

10. A husband wants to leave property to his wife, with the children to get whatever is left when she dies. But that means two estate taxes on substantially the same property: on his property when he dies and on what is left when his widow dies. He sets up a trust for the benefit of his wife, the trust to terminate and to distribute its properties to the children when she dies. Now there is only one estate tax, because what she will own when she dies is merely a life interest, with no value as of the moment of her death. Such a trust might qualify as qualified terminable interest property, giving the executor the right to claim a marital deduction for it if he/she sees fit.

11. An individual would like to part with some property so that it won't be part of his estate when he dies and at the same time create an annual income-tax deduction for himself. For example, a physician owns the building in which he practices. He transfers this property to a trust for the benefit of his children. But he needs the building for his practice, so he leases it back from the trust, the rent being a business deduction for him. (See Chapter Nineteen, "Sale-and-Leaseback.")

12. An individual wants his widowed daughter-in-law to have an income for as long as she doesn't remarry. He transfers income-producing securities to a trust for her benefit, the trust to terminate and to transfer the principal according to his instruction if she remarries.

13. A father wishes to set up a trust for the benefit of his several children or grandchildren. The trustee is given instructions or discretionary

power to apportion trust principal for the beneficiaries—typically, when one of the children marries, or has a child, or undergoes surgery, or needs to maintain her standard of living if she marries an unestablished artist, or remains with the family business that the other children have abandoned as unglamorous, or wishes to go into business, or seeks to go to medical school. But the father doesn't want any child to know how the others have participated in his wealth. He sets up individual trusts, each with a separate trustee and instructions or discretionary powers. On requisition by each trustee, funds are provided by a "pourover" trust established by the father. Now none of the beneficiaries can find out what the others are getting.

14. A person wants to ensure that her pet animals are well provided for when she dies, but she can't be certain that her executor (an individual or a bank) will be cooperative. She sets up a trust for the benefit of her pets, choosing a trustee who is sympathetic to her wishes.

15. When an individual gets older, he may fear that he will lose his business or investment judgment without realizing it. He is concerned lest his failing abilities deprive him of the property or income that he needs. He transfers this property to a trust with a competent trustee for his own benefit. Because the trust property is being used for his own benefit, he will be taxed on its income. But he has made certain that he won't dissipate the principal.

16. Someone has been making contributions to her favorite church, charity, college, hospital, etc., for many years. She would like to have the contributions continue in her name for all time, or for a period of years;

for example, until the new library building is completely financed. Income-producing properties are transferred to a trust for this purpose.

17. A husband wants to leave his wife the largest amount that will take full advantage of the marital deduction. (See Chapter Fourteen, "The Marital Deduction.") How much should he leave her in order to minimize taxes in both their estates? By will he can leave amounts to a trustee that will qualify, in whole or in part, as qualified terminable interest property. His executor, after his death, can decide what portion of this trust should pass, estate-tax-free, to his wife under the marital deduction, and what portion should be taxable in his estate in order to take full advantage of the unified estate- and gift-tax credit.

18. An immigrant who has become financially successful in the United States wishes to leave money to the European town in which he was born. No deduction is allowed for a charitable bequest to a foreign political subdivision. But a bequest is deductible when made to a United States trust for purely charitable purposes, such as doing good works in his place of birth.

19. An individual is distressed by the many demands made on her by charitable organizations. She seeks peace of mind by transferring proper-ties to a trust that she establishes for benevolent purposes. Then when requests are made to her, she can say, "Speak to the trustees. They now have sole discretion as to contributions."

20. Trusts may be a vehicle for providing a life income to a designated person (such as the grantor), with the principal going to a charitable organization subject to this life interest. (See Chapter Seven, "Charitable Remainder Trusts.")

A grantor is treated as holding any power or interest that was held by an individual who either (1) was the grantor's spouse at the time the power or interest was created or (2) became the grantor's spouse subsequent to the creation of that power or interest.

There now are income tax brackets for trusts that retain income, for example, for ultimate distribution to the children of the person creating the trust—Revenue Reconciliation Act of 1993.

Conclusions and advice

• You must let go of any meaningful incident of ownership of trust properties. That includes the right to say how much each beneficiary receives annually, even though you don't exercise this right and nothing can come back to you personally in any event. And bear in mind that renunciation of incidents of ownership made within three years of death will not keep the value of the property out of your estate, even though absolute gifts within that period are generally no longer included in your estate.

• Remember that a trust may be used for your own benefit as well as that of other beneficiaries. But you will be taxed on any benefits for yourself.

• Trusts are created under state law; therefore, have your trust set up by a lawyer who is familiar with the laws of the state in which it is created. For example, will a spendthrift trust be recognized there?

The primary grantor and the primary beneficiary are the key to all IRS tax determinations. Thus:

• Two or more trusts are treated as one if (1) they have substantially the same grantor(s) or primary beneficiary(ies) and (2) the trusts' principal purpose is to avoid federal income tax.

- A couple is treated as a single grantor or beneficiary.

In the case of married persons, the unified credit may not be fully available to each spouse upon that person's death if his own assets are not large enough. For example, if this credit is an amount up to $600,000 but one spouse dies with assets of less than that amount, the difference will be lost, whereas the other spouse may have assets valued at more than $600,000 but will be limited to the $600,000 credit. The solution: each spouse should transfer to this trust for the benefit of the other an amount equal to the excess of the largest sum which may pass tax-free after application of all credits over the value of any property otherwise passing under his will that are included in his gross estate. This "credit equivalent trust" will be labelled as a pecuniary bequest and not a fractional part of his estate. Provision may be made for payments by the trustee of whatever trust income she requires during her lifetime or, alternatively, of amounts of trust income within stipulated limits.

- A trust may be used so that there is no interruption in the operation of a plan to distribute assets, inasmuch as one's time of death customarily is not known and it can be very sudden. It has been pointed out that the time of one's death can be known so as to implement estate planning only where his birth certificate contains an expiration date.

Chapter Four

THE SHORT-TERM TRUST

Prior to the Tax Reform Act of 1986, the short-term trust was useful because it allowed a donor to part with property and its income during a period when the person was in a high tax bracket and didn't need the income. At the end of a period of time (over 10 years minimum), the trust ended and the property returned to the donor. Such a trust was considered a benevolent boomerang that could return when needed.

But generally in the case of transfers in trust made after March 1, 1986, the income of a trust is taxed to its grantor if the trust principal will return to him or his spouse at any time. An exception is provided where the principal may return only after the death of an income beneficiary of the trust who is a lineal descendant of the grantor. And an exception to this new rule is made for certain trusts created under a binding property settlement entered into before March 1, 1986.

Nature of a short-term trust

This type of plan involves what is sometimes called a "come-back" or "give-and-keep" trust.

An individual transfers income-producing properties, such as securities or real estate, to a trust for the benefit of someone else—a person or an institution—who will receive all the income. The duration of the trust is selected by the grantor according to his own purposes, but it must be for more than 10 years. He will have the satisfaction of seeing what would have been his taxable income go to a relative or friend, who is usually in a lower tax bracket. Such a trust may be set up in order to provide for the education of a child. At the end of the stated duration of the trust (such as where the income beneficiary may be expected to be sufficiently successful in his business or profession so that he no longer requires this assistance), the trust terminates and the remaining principal goes to a predetermined party or parties, who cannot be the grantor or his spouse.

Reversionary interests

An individual may set up a trust to provide income to his adult lineal descendant, such as his daughter or his granddaughter, for life. He transfers income-producing properties to a trust, which will give its income to her for as long as she lives, after which the trust will terminate and the properties will return ("revert") to him—or to his estate should he die before the income beneficiary does. There is a pitfall here. A grantor may be treated as the owner of a trust in which he has a reversionary interest in either the principal or income—and taxed on the income. This can happen if, at the time the trust is created, the grantor's interest will or may be reasonably expected to take effect in repossession or enjoyment *if* there is any significant possibility that interests or powers may become effective in the grantor *and* there is more than a 5 percent possibility that any of the proscribed powers or interests will become effective to the grantor after the transfer of the property to the trust. For this purpose, the possibility that an interest may return to the grantor or his spouse solely under intestacy laws is to be ignored.

The value of the reversionary interest, if any, is determined by comparing the actuarial possibility that a transferred right might be subject to return to the grantor—for example, if the grantee should die before the grantor does. The possibility of any reversionary interest can be eliminated entirely by provision that upon the death of the grantee, any remaining interest will go to named contingent or secondary parties, such as a non-profit organization.

Life expectancies for this purpose are based on published statistical data.

Federal gift tax

The transfer of property to a short-term trust may result in federal gift tax based on the value of the life income transferred to the life tenant. The gift tax applies to the total value of the property transferred, not merely to the value of the income interest, because it will vary. In addition, the $10,000 per donee annual gift-tax exclusion is not available, as this applies only to property of ascertainable value.

You can't change it

A grantor may not retain power to modify the agreement. Nor can he/she have any special privilege, such as the right to borrow from the trust principal without adequate security.

Federal estate tax

Because the grantor of a short-term trust that is still in existence at the time of his death has something of value when he dies, it will be includable in his gross estate. His estate will not include the full value of the property he has transferred, because he has no ownership of the income interest. The value of the property is reduced by the actuarial value of the right to the income possessed by the income beneficiary at the time of the grantor's death. The reversionary right possessed by the decedent at the time of his death must be discounted, because the principal that will return to the estate after the trust terminates (for example, 13 years later) must reflect the fact that a dollar paid in 13 years will be worth less than a dollar paid today.

An individual's gross estate includes the value of transfer in trust whereby he will get back the property transferred by surviving the life tenant, if the decedent had at least a 5 percent reversionary interest. To determine whether or not the decedent retained a reversionary interest in the transferred property of a value in excess of 5 percent, the value of the reversionary interest is compared with the value of the transferred interests that are not dependent upon survivorship of the decedent. The greater the age of the life tenant, the lower the value of the reversionary interest. The transferor can reduce or even eliminate the value of the reversionary interest by providing that, on the death of the life tenant, his interest will be passed to a named third party. This could be a charitable organization with unlimited life.

Conclusions and advice

• In setting up a short-term trust, consider carefully whether you can do without the income, taking into account every economic, social, and personal factor you can imagine, including: the possibility of an increase in the number of your dependents; their needs, real and potential; inflation and the state of the economy; the possibility of extraordinary medical expenses; the possibility of severe economic reverses for your industry, company, or investments; even the possibility of the loss of your employment.

• The trust principal cannot revert to the grantor or to his spouse, except where this reversion applies in the case of a lineal descendant.

• Consult an experienced professional on establishing a short-term trust that has such a reversionary interest. The valuation of such a trust can be quite complex, and without proper planning, the available benefits can be lost.

• Do not retain any power to alter the trust arrangement.

• Do not expect to avoid federal gift tax by transferring property to a trust rather than to an individual.

• Do not consider the health of the life tenant in computing the value of a reversionary interest. Actuarial tables must be used.

• Sometimes it may be desirable to set up a trust even when you know you'll be taxed on its income. The income-producing property you transfer to this trust is owned by the trustee you have named, which can be yourself. When you die, the property goes to persons you have selected to be the recipients. Inasmuch as this *living trust* customary is revocable by you at any time until you die or become disabled, you are taxed on the trust income. But trust property is not subject to the delay, expense, and publicity of probate, for it is not part of your estate.

Chapter Five

GENERATION-SKIPPING TRUSTS

A device that was favored for many years for avoiding payment of estate tax on transfers of property along generational lines was a trust that left a life interest to the grantor's children, with either a further life interest or a distribution to the grandchildren, great-grandchildren, and so on down the line. This "generation-skipping trust" had a major advantage: Because it was only a life interest, the property of the grantor's child was not taxed to his estate at his death; the value was transmitted entirely to the next younger generation.

However, the loophole that permitted this kind of tax avoidance was closed in 1976, when Congress imposed a "skip-a-generation" tax. In effect, it made the distribution of trust assets to two or more generations of heirs subject to a tax equal to what the escaped estate tax would have been.

Subsequently this was repealed by a new law that was retroactive to

1976. Because of the complexity of the provisions and the confusing legislative history, it is advisable to discuss specific problems with competent professional counsel if you contemplate a skip-a-generation arrangement. Transfers to one's spouse are not covered by the tax because the spouses are considered to be of the same generation, regardless of differences in age.

There is a flat-rate tax on both (1) transfers under a trust or similar arrangement involving benefit sharing by more than one generation below that of the grantor and (2) direct beneficiaries more than one generation below that of the grantor (that is, which skip generations). This tax is imposed on taxable terminations and taxable distributions (including distributions of income) under generation-skipping arrangements. A skip person must be a "natural person" whose generation assignment is two or more generations below that of the transferor. Taxable beneficiaries include only persons having interests in (as opposed to powers over) property.

The use of trust property to satisfy any obligation of support arising by reason of state law is disregarded in determining whether a portion may be distributed to, or for the benefit of, a person other than the beneficiary of the gift if this use is discretionary or pursuant to any state law substantially equivalent to the Uniform Gifts to Minors Act. (See Chapter Eleven, "The Uniform Gifts to Minors Act.") Thus, a parent is not treated as having an interest in a trust if the trust instrument requires that trust assets be used to discharge a support obligation.

Rules similar to those governing the deduction of administration expenses, indebtedness, and taxes for income and estate purposes have been extended to the generation-skipping tax. Thus, these amounts are generally not deductible in determining taxable income unless an election is made not to deduct these amounts in determining the taxable income subject to the generation-skipping tax.

There is a specific exemption of $1,000,000 per transferor, with transfers in excess of that amount subject to tax at the maximum gift- and estate-tax equivalent. No allocation of any portion of this exemption may be made to any property that is transferred by the transferor during his lifetime but would be includable in his gross estate (except transactions within three years of his death) until the end of the estate-tax inclusion period. That term means the period that would be includable in the transferor's gross estate if he had died. The term "transferor" includes the transferor of any property includable in a person's estate or with respect to which he has made a gift.

In order to qualify for the trust exception, the assets of a trust that terminates on the beneficiary's death must be includable in the beneficiary's estate.

Property transferred to an incompetent person after August 3, 1990, is now subject to the generation-skipping tax.

A credit against the generation-skipping transfer tax is permitted equal to 5 percent of any state taxes on generation-skipping transfers.

Alternatives

There are circumstances under which an individual may find it necessary to provide a life income to a beneficiary through a trust, the property to go to persons in a second younger generation on the death of the income beneficiary. Obviously this will mean imposition of the generation-skipping transfer tax when the life tenant dies. But there are times when the tax consequences should be ignored.

If a person is concerned about the generation-skipping transfer tax, he might provide for his second generation of beneficiaries through the medium of life insurance. Or he could establish completely separate trusts, one for the children and one for the grandchildren.

Conclusions and advice

• Because of the technicalities of the generation-skipping tax, consult a professional adviser wherever two or more tiers of beneficiaries are involved.

• Do not assume that skip-a-generation trusts are inadvisable merely because a transfer tax must be paid. The trust may still be highly desirable for nontax reasons.

• Do not seek to tie up your assets in trust for an extended period of time. Many states have laws against perpetuities: They may allow you to make provision only for the extent of a life or lives already in being at the time the trust is created, plus 21 years.

• A dozen or so states impose a generation-skipping tax.

• Under the Omnibus Budget Reconciliation Act of 1993, the generation-skipping tax rate is 55%.

Chapter Six

SPENDTHRIFT TRUSTS

You wish to provide for your son during his lifetime, but you want him to be the actual beneficiary. If you have reason to suspect that he will run up huge debts or otherwise waste his inheritance, you can set up a spendthrift trust for him. Courts have held that the grantor of property to a trust has the right to protect the beneficiary against his own voluntary improvidence or financial misfortune. The property that is to produce the beneficiary's income is never his; therefore neither he nor his creditors can squander it.

How it works

A trust is set up and furnished with income-producing assets. The trustee, a bank or other independent fiduciary, is given discretion as to when, under what circumstances, and in what amounts to pay out the income. Provision may be made that if the trustee isn't satisfied that the beneficiary will be using the money for what the trust agreement and correlative instructions have defined as normal living expenses and pleasures, no money will be paid out at that time. If the trust instrument provides that income is to be paid out for support, the son may go to court to argue that he is not getting enough to meet that test, especially if he is still of the age where his parents are legally obliged to support him. If the arrangement was created by will and the parents are dead, their obligation of support is nebulous, and in any case, most spendthrift trusts are created for persons of legal age. Ordinarily, the trustee can't be compelled to pay out anything more than, in his sole discretion, he feels is appropriate. A line of persistent creditors cannot change the trustee's mind if discretionary powers have been bestowed. Nor can trust principal be touched by the son or his creditors, for the principal is being held by the trustee for the benefit of a specified remainderman. However, if the son's estate has been named to be remainderman, creditors may seek to attach the son's remainder interest. Income that is not paid out by the watchful trustee under his discretionary powers may, in accordance with the trust agreement, be paid out at such future time, if ever, as the trustee deems appropriate. Or undistributed income may be made part of the trust principal if that is the way the trust instrument was written.

Actual language used in trust instruments

Here is the wording of one spendthrift trust that a court recognized as having accomplished its intended purpose:

"The Trustees shall pay or apply for the benefit of my son ... so much of the net income of said trust, up to the whole thereof, as the Trustees may from time to time deem necessary or advisable for his proper care, maintenance and support. The balance of said net income, if any, shall be accumulated by the Trustees, and from time to time added to the principal of the trust estate."

Here the trustees had the discretionary authority, and perhaps some further guidelines, to determine what was "necessary" for the beneficiary's proper care, maintenance, and support.

In some instances a grantor seeks to prevent the beneficiary's creditors from attaching amounts otherwise payable to the beneficiary by such language as "that said trustee shall pay the net income therefrom in monthly installments ... during his life, and not into the hands of any other person, whether claiming by his authority or otherwise."

In one case, the trust agreement declared:

"Each and every beneficiary under this trust is hereby restrained from and shall be without right, power, or authority to sell, transfer, pledge, mortgage, hypothecate, alienate, anticipate or in any other manner affect or impair his, her or their beneficial and legal rights, titles, interests, and estates in and to the income and/or principal of this trust during the entire term thereof; nor shall the rights, titles, interests, and estates of any beneficiary hereunder be subject to the rights or claims of creditors of any beneficiary, and all the income and/or principal of this trust shall be transferrable, payable and deliverable solely to the beneficiaries as herein provided, and the Trustees may require the personal receipt of any beneficiary as a condition precedent to the payment of any money or other property to such beneficiary."

This provision was held to be legal under the laws of the state in which it was drawn. But under another section of this same law, ordinary creditors were permitted to reach all income of a beneficiary of such a provision except so much as was necessary for his support and education.

Some trust instruments contain an outright forfeiture provision of the beneficiary's rights if he takes any steps that are contrary to the grantor's instructions that the money not be available to other parties. One agreement provided for the forfeiture of a beneficiary's rights "if from any cause whatsoever the said income or principal, or any part thereof, shall, or but for this proviso, would at any time become payable to or for the benefit of any person, firm, association, corporation, political subdivision, state or federal government, other than such beneficiary."

Effect of state law

Counsel should check the state law to determine whether spendthrift trusts will be recognized in that jurisdiction in the face of creditors' claims. Some states regard spendthrift trusts as a fraud against the creditors. Usually a gambling debt is not regarded as a valid and enforceable claim under state law.

The language of a trust instrument or of a state law does not apply to the Internal Revenue Service. So even if trust income can be withheld by the trustee under his discretionary powers, and neither the beneficiary nor his creditors can reach this money, that most persistent of all creditors, the IRS, is not bound by the wording of private agreements or of the law of a particular state.

Federal gift tax

If a spendthrift trust agreement provides that the trustee is to have discretion to decide whether trust income should be distributed to a beneficiary in a particular year, this is not a present interest that would qualify a donor's transfers to the trust for the annual $10,000 per donee gift-tax exclusion.

Who is the spendthrift?

A grantor may not be concerned so much that his son or daughter has spendthrift tendencies, as that this person's spouse is the one who is likely to be wildly extravagant or gullible. The grantor may provide that anything he gives or leaves to his son or daughter is to be in the form of a life income from a trust, so that the principal cannot get into the hands of the spouse. The remainderman or remaindermen will be specified as the grantor sees fit—often the grandchildren rather than the prodigal spouse are named.

Encouragement not to be a spendthrift

A grantor may seek to convert a spendthrift trust into an incentive trust. Provision may be made so that the trustee is empowered to supplement authorized or mandatory support payments with additional trust income to equal what the beneficiary has earned in any year through his/her own efforts.

Conclusions and advice

• Check with counsel as to whether a spendthrift trust is valid in your state or is deemed to be a fraud against creditors.

• A spendthrift trust may be used to protect principal from the beneficiary's spouse.

• The trustee may be empowered to pay out to the spendthrift beneficiary any additional amounts to match what the latter was able to earn by his/her own efforts.

• Do not seek to protect a beneficiary from claims by the IRS. It can't be done.

• Do not treat transfers to a spendthrift trust as gifts of present interests if the trustee has discretionary powers as to the time of payouts.

Chapter Seven

CHARITABLE REMAINDER TRUSTS

A husband wishes to provide an income for life to a designated party, such as his spouse. He chooses not to give her income-producing properties, for she may not want the responsibility of investments and fund management. Nor does he desire her to have the properties at the time of her death, for they might then go to persons whom he doesn't wish to receive what he is still apt to think of as "my property." Instead, when his principal beneficiary dies, he would like to have the assets go to his favorite charity or hospital, or to his alma mater. He'd like this even better if he could get some tax deductions. If he plans properly, he can.

Charitable deductions

For federal income-, gift-, and estate-tax purposes, deduction is allowed for a charitable gift of a remainder interest in a trust where there is a non-charitable income beneficiary if the trust is either a charitable remainder annuity trust or a charitable remainder unitrust. The amount receivable each year by the income beneficiary must be either a stated dollar amount or a fixed percentage of the value of the trust property.

The grantor is entitled to a federal income-tax deduction for the actuarial value of the remainder interest that will pass to the designated charitable organization. This deduction is taken in the tax year of the transfer to the trust. When the grantor dies, the value of the remainder interest passing to the charitable organization is deductible as a charitable bequest for federal tax purposes.

What the income beneficiary receives

An annuity trust must be required by the trust instrument to distribute at least 5 percent of the net fair market value of its assets each year, as valued at the time of the donor's contribution. Income payments must be made at least annually.

A unitrust must be required by the trust instrument to distribute yearly at least 5 percent of the net fair market value of its assets, valued annually, or the amount of the trust income, excluding capital gains, whichever is lower.

In valuing the amount of the charitable contribution, the deduction is computed on the basis that the income beneficiary of the trust will receive the amounts specified. No provision may exist for payments to noncharitable beneficiaries of amounts other than the stated annuity or fixed percentage amount. Principal may not be diverted under any circumstances to a noncharitable beneficiary.

Available options

The income interest in the case of both forms of trust may be either for a term of years or for the life of the income beneficiary. A charitable annuity trust or unitrust may have more than one noncharitable beneficiary if the interest of such beneficiary is either for a term of years, not to exceed 20, or is for the life of the beneficiary. An individual who was not living at the time of creation of the trust, however, may not be an income beneficiary of a charitable remainder trust.

The governing instrument of a unitrust may provide that when the trust income is less than the required payment to the noncharitable income beneficiary, the trust need distribute to him only the amount of the trust income. The deficiencies in income distributions in this case (that is, where the trust income was less than the stated amount payable to the income beneficiary) must be made up in later years when the trust income exceeds the amount otherwise payable to the income beneficiary for that year. The determination of what constitutes trust income is made under the applicable state law and may not include such items as capital gains, which must be allocated to the trust principal.

Federal income-tax treatment

Under either an annuity trust or a unitrust, amounts paid to the income beneficiary are treated as consisting of the following:

1. Ordinary income, to the extent of the trust's ordinary income for the taxable year and its undistributed ordinary income from prior years.

2. Capital gain, to the extent of the trust's capital gains for the year and undistributed capital gains (determined on a cumulative net basis)

from prior years.

3. Other income (such as state bond interest), to the extent of the trust's other income for the year and its undistributed other income from prior years.

4. Distribution of principal.

A charitable remainder trust that qualifies as an annuity trust or a unitrust is exempt from federal income tax except on what may be characterized as unrelated business income from sources outside the stated purpose of the trust. An example: rent or royalties from a subsidiary of a business interest acquired by the trust.

Pooled income funds

One type of gift of charitable remainder interest in trust involves a transfer of property to a pooled income fund. This is a trust to which a person has transferred property, giving an irrevocable remainder interest in the property to a public charity and retaining an income interest in the property for the life of one or more beneficiaries living at the time of the transfer. There are a number of restrictions on a pooled income fund, including the following:

• The fund must commingle the property transferred to it with properties transferred to it under similar circumstances by other persons.

• The fund may have no investments in tax-exempt securities.

• No donor or income beneficiary may be a trustee of the fund, and the fund must be maintained by the charitable organization to which the remainder interest is given.

• Each person with a life interest in the pooled income fund must receive an annual income determined by the trust's rate of return for the year.

A pooled income fund won't qualify if it includes amounts received under types of arrangement other than those described above; however, a pooled income fund that is commingled with other, larger groups of assets for investment purposes may have a separate accounting for the fund's assets.

The amount of the charitable contribution deduction allowed the donor upon transfer of the property to a pooled income fund is determined by valuing the interest income on the basis of the highest annual rate of return earned by the fund in any of the three years preceding the transfer. If a fund has not been in existence for this period of time, the rate of return is assumed to be 6 percent unless a different rate is prescribed by the Secretary of the Treasury or the Internal Revenue Service.

Giving up the charitable deduction

It was noted that the charitable deduction is allowed only if there is no right of invasion; that is, no right to use principal for the benefit of the noncharitable income beneficiary. But on occasion it may be desirable to allow for a right of invasion in order to achieve other objectives, even though the tax advantage is lost.

Conclusions and advice

• Despite changes in the tax law, you can still get a charitable deduction for the value of a remainder interest after your beneficiary receives a life income. But the conditions under which this is possible are so limited that you should seek guidance from an attorney, accountant, or trust officer.

• Trust income is based on actuarial factors, so advice on the computation involved is important.

• Consult counsel on what constitutes trust income in a particular state.

• Do not provide for the use of principal to meet extraordinary medical or other needs of the noncharitable income beneficiary.

• Do not overlook the possible advantage of naming more than one life beneficiary.

Chapter Eight

GIFTS STILL
HAVE ADVANTAGES

Prior to 1977, the federal gift-tax rate was only three-fourths of the federal estate-tax rate at each value bracket. This differential encouraged the making of lifetime gifts rather than property dispositions by will. Now the tax rates are the same, and there is a unified credit for both taxes. That has led to a general tendency to think, "Why should I give away property now when the tax impact will be no greater if I hold on to what's mine until I die? The longer I keep my properties, the longer I can keep my options open."

Why lifetime transfers may be more attractive than transfers by will

There is some superficial appeal to this thinking. But there are persuasive tax and other reasons for making lifetime transfers rather than transfers by will, starting right now. Here are the principal reasons:

1. If property seems likely to appreciate in value, a transfer will have less tax impact now than it would if made later when fair market value is higher.

2. Some property automatically becomes more valuable each year. For example, if you give away a policy of insurance on your life, gift tax is based upon the interpolated terminal reserve, which for practical purposes may be thought of as the cash surrender value. Assuming that you do not borrow against the policy, the reserve that is the basis for gift-tax value will increase each year. The longer you wait to give away the policy, the higher the gift tax will be.

3. The donor can reduce his current federal income tax by making transfers of income-producing properties to beneficiaries.

4. In many situations, a present gift of property will save the donor all liability for state or local property taxes. Many localities have intangible property taxes on securities, receivables, and sometimes bank accounts.

5. A present gift of property can save the donor administration, custody, and insurance expenses, plus the chores of property ownership.

6. There is an annual gift-tax exclusion of up to $10,000 per donee, which can be doubled to as much as $20,000 if both spouses consent to the making of a gift. The sooner such a program starts, the more there is that can be given away free of tax.

7. The gift-tax marital deduction allows transfers to a spouse (including a nonresident one) without tax liability.

There is a $100,000 annual exclusion for transfers by gift to a noncitizen spouse in the case of transfers that would qualify for the marital deduction if the donee were a US citizen. A transfer to a noncitizen spouse that creates a joint tenancy is treated as consideration belonging to the surviving spouse if the transfer would have constituted a gift had the donor been a US citizen. Accordingly, the amount of joint tenancy property included in the estate of the first spouse to die is reduced proportionately by the amount of the gift.

8. Gain on the sale of appreciated-value property can be avoided by selling the property to a beneficiary at cost, making a gift of the balance.

9. Gifts can be made of property that has appreciated in value, so that the donor is relieved of the built-in gain on appreciation on which he would have to pay tax if he sold the property.

10. Lifetime gifts can reduce the cost of administering what will eventually be the donor's gross estate, since executors' fees are customarily based upon the size of the estate.

11. Lifetime transfers can minimize the chance of loss of the donor's property. A physician might be sued for malpractice in an amount that exceeds his liability insurance coverage, which would make his other property subject to creditors' claims. Bona fide gifts to beneficiaries would protect this property.

12. A donor's dispositions at the present time might better represent what he really wants to do than transfers made at a time when he might lack today's acumen and resistance to external pressures.

13. By making modest gifts of income-producing property or business interests at this time, a donor gains the opportunity to see how responsibly his beneficiaries behave in the management of this property. If they prove incompetent to handle it, he might modify his will to leave them money

instead, or to place property in trust for them, with a competent and knowledgeable party as the fiduciary.

14. Lifetime gifts can be made with assurance that no one will learn about them other than the donees themselves and the IRS, the latter being bound by law to keep tax information confidential. What is left to anyone by will, on the other hand, is hardly a secret, for wills are available in probate courts or other designated offices where anyone can read them.

15. Gifts made at this time won't be held up in probate proceedings or by the slowness of an executor.

16. Gifts made at the present time can afford the donor the psychological satisfaction of seeing his beneficiaries enjoy them.

Conclusions and advice

• Remember that your children, grandchildren, or parents may possess something of great tax value: low income-tax brackets. But unearned income of a child under 14 can now be taxed at the parents' marginal tax rates. (See Item 16 in "Hidden Traps in Estate Planning.") Includable in a parent's gross estate when he/she dies is the value of property where the parent transfers an existing enterprise or assets from that enterprise to another one in which a child owns a disproportionately large share of potential appreciation and in which the parent retains an income interest or other right.

• Be certain that your gifts are complete, or the property may end up in your gross estate after all. Have you complied with the laws of some states that require real-estate transfers in written form?

• Have you retained control over property that you have transferred?

• Generally we don't know when we are going to die. But lifetime gifts may well be planned in the light of what we do know. For example, a sensible annual physical checkup may alert someone to the fact that he'd better accelerate his gift program with all deliberate speed.

• Be careful not to make gifts of income-producing properties if it leaves you without adequate livelihood. Anticipate your needs in light of inflation, and presume that as you get older, medical expenses will increase—unless you carry a really good major-medical insurance policy.

• Do not make gifts that will relieve you of a legal obligation without being aware of all the tax consequences. If you make a gift of income-producing property to a trust for the benefit of your minor child, and this income is used to provide maintenance of the child, you have been relieved of a legal obligation. So the trust principal can end up in your gross estate. Trust principal where the trust is for the benefit of a minor child won't be includable in your estate if you have not been relieved of a legal obligation because you have made other arrangements for the child's support requirements.

• Do not make lifetime gifts after you have used up your unified estate- and gift-tax credit. This would be equivalent to prepayment of estate taxes.

• If a marriage appears to be strained, a husband and wife should not make split gifts. This could result in one spouse being held responsible for the entire gift-tax liability even if some or all of the property really had been that of the other spouse.

• If a person has an annuity payable to him for the remainder of his life, and he has this changed to a contract calling for payments (in a lesser amount) to himself and a named person (such as his wife) for as long a period as she may outlive him, he has made a taxable gift to her.

Chapter Nine

TAKING ADVANTAGE OF THE ANNUAL EXCLUSION

Lifetime transfers of property are subject to the same tax rates as transfers by will. But the first $10,000 of gifts to any single donee in each calendar year is excluded from taxable lifetime transfers. And if the donee's spouse elects to share in the gift, the annual exclusion can be brought up to $20,000 per donee.

Eligibility for the annual exclusion

Gifts are eligible for this annual exclusion if they fulfill the following conditions: The value of the interest transferred must be reasonably certain, and what is transferred must be a present as opposed to a future interest. A gift without reasonably ascertainable value might be a transfer of an income interest in shares of a family corporation at a time when dividends could not be paid and the shares could not be sold or otherwise converted into cash. The transfer of a franchise would not be excludable if its value could not be determined because of unpredictable income, which itself was subject to various restrictions. To qualify as a present interest, a gift must carry an unrestricted right to the immediate use, possession, or enjoyment of property or its income (for example, income from certain land for the remainder of the donee's life or for a specified number of years). A promise to make a gift in the future is not a present interest, even though the promise may be an enforceable one. A future interest is one that is to commence in use, possession, or enjoyment at some later date or time. The question of time, not when the donee gets title but when he/she gets the use, possession, or enjoyment of the property, is what is decisive.

The gift of a life insurance policy where the donee has no rights until the death of the insured is a future interest, and is not excludable from taxable gifts. If a donor conveys realty to a donee but reserves the right to the rentals for as long as he/she lives, the gift is of a future interest. The donee's possession and enjoyment of the land is postponed until the death of the donor.

Where spouse is not a US citizen

The $10,000 annual exclusion is not available where the donor spouse is a US citizen but the donee spouse is not. There is a $100,000 annual exclusion for transfers by gift to a noncitizen spouse in the case of transfers that would qualify for the marital deduction if the donee were a US citizen. For example, a gift in trust does not qualify for the $100,000 annual exclusion unless it is within one of the exceptions to the terminable-interest rule. This rule applies to gifts made after June 29, 1989.

A nonresident is entitled to a marital deduction or annual exclusion for gift-tax purposes in the same circumstances as a US citizen or resident. Thus, gifts from a nonresident noncitizen to a US-citizen spouse qualify for the marital deduction. In addition, each year the first $100,000 in gifts from a nonresident noncitizen to a noncitizen spouse is not taxed, as long as the gifts would qualify for the marital deduction if the donee were a US citizen. The deduction and annual exclusion apply only if the property is subject to US gift tax.

Unutilized exclusions are forfeited

Unlike charitable contributions and business losses, unutilized gift-tax exclusions cannot be carried over for use in a later year's computations. So if the annual exclusion is not fully utilized in any single year, it is forfeited forever. That places a great premium on timing. The earlier you start an annual gift program, the greater will be the potential dollar benefits of the annual exclusion. If you lack the cash to make gifts in a particular year, you might consider borrowing money for the purpose. And the gift need not be in cash if property with a determinable value is given for immediate enjoyment.

Available donees

There is no limit on the number of beneficiaries who may receive gifts subject to the annual exclusion. Plural donees could build up the amount of the exclusion indefinitely. In the case of gifts in trust, the beneficiaries are the donees. Transfers to several trusts for the benefit of the same beneficiary, however, permit only one $10,000 exclusion that year. If gifts are made to the donor's son, to the wife of the donor's son, and to the married couple jointly, there are only two exclusions, as only two individuals are involved. Each of two brothers made gifts at the same time to his own children and to his brother's children (the donor's nieces and nephews), but the gifts to the nieces and nephews didn't qualify as separate exclusions, being regarded in this situation as indirect gifts to each donor's own children. Reciprocal or cross-gift arrangements, however intricately structured, are similarly not recognized for separate exclusions.

Gifts to minors may qualify as present interests

Under appropriate circumstances, a gift to or for the benefit of a minor child qualifies as a gift of a present interest even though the child does not actually have the use, possession, or enjoyment of the gift. There must be a provision that the property and any income from it may be expended by or for the benefit of the donee before he reaches age 21, and will to the extent not so expended either pass to the child on reaching 21 or be payable to the child's estate or to any person who has been designated in case the minor dies before attaining age 21.

Gift-splitting

The amount of the annual gift-tax exclusion can in effect be doubled to as much as $20,000 per donee per year if the proper election is made. A gift by one spouse to someone other than his or her spouse may be treated as made one-half by each spouse, but only if each was a citizen or resident of the US at the time of the gift.

As a general rule, this split-gift election can be made only on the federal gift-tax return filed by the 15th day of the fourth month following the close of the year in which the gift is made. The consent may not be signified after a notice of deficiency with respect to tax for the year is sent by the Internal Revenue Service to either spouse.

Once the gift-tax return is filed, even though the consent had been overlooked because of an error of judgment or lack of knowledge of the requirements, the consent can't be given in any other way. In a few isolated instances, courts have allowed gift-splitting even where the election had not been made in the required form, on the ground that proper gift-splitting consents had been filed on returns for the preceding years, and in this particular year the donor's accountant testified that his clients told him that they intended their gifts to be split. But don't count on receiving this lenient treatment from a court if no election is filed.

The only acceptable way to make the split-gift election is to check the block headed "yes" on Form 709, "United States Gift Tax Return." This is one response to the question, "Do you consent to have the gifts made by you and by your spouse to third parties during the calendar year considered as made one-half by each of you?" If no gift-tax return is filed for any reason, clearly no election can be made.

Where the consent is effective for the entire year, all gifts made by husband or wife to third parties during that year must be treated in the same way.

Recapitalization in order to utilize the annual exclusion

An individual may feel that he must sacrifice the annual gift-tax exclusion if substantially all of his wealth is tied up in his closely held corporation. He doesn't want to give away his stock because its voting power is essential to him in controlling the enterprise. But a gift to take advantage of the exclusion is possible. He can cause a recapitalization to be effected from his present one-class voting stock into voting and nonvoting shares. The latter can then be given away as he sees fit—for example, by presents each year of enough of the nonvoting stock to meet the annual exclusion rules. (See Chapter Thirteen, "Using a Corporation to Transfer Assets.")

Conclusions and advice

• Start your gift program as soon as possible in order to maximize the number of annual exclusions.

• The amount of the exclusion is effectively doubled if your spouse consents to participate in gift-splitting, even if in fact she has no property to give away.

• If you feel you have no property to give away, borrow from a bank so as not to waste the annual exclusion. Or have a recapitalization of the corporation where your wealth is tied up so that you can give away shares without loss of control.

• Do not make gifts of future interests if you would qualify for the annual exclusion.

• Do not seek to gain annual exclusions by working up a deal with a relative or a friend—"You make gifts of $10,000 to each of my children and I'll make similar gifts to each of yours." Reciprocal or cross-gifts don't provide additional exclusions.

Chapter Ten

GIFTS TO MINORS CAN QUALIFY FOR THE ANNUAL EXCLUSION

As noted, the first $10,000 of gifts to any individual in a given year is not subject to federal gift tax, nor does it use up any of the unified credit for gift and estate taxes. But this annual exclusion applies only to gifts of present interests—that is, where there is an unrestricted right to the immediate use, possession, or enjoyment of the property given. The exclusion doesn't apply to the gift of a future interest. This would appear to eliminate the exclusion of gifts to minor children, who, for legal or practical reasons, are in no position to handle the immediate right to do as they please with a gift of cash, diamonds, postage stamps, or antique firearms. A special provision in the tax law, however, permits the annual gift-tax exclusion even in cases when a minor child may not be able to get his/her hands on the property, or determine what is going to be done with it, for another 15 years.

Start your gift-tax program when children are still young

Careful adherence to this rule means that you can begin to take advantage of the annual exclusion when a baby is born, giving away substantial amounts free of tax by the time the child reaches age 21, without fear that the recipient will squander or misuse the property while still financially unsophisticated. Of course, this advantage is multiplied when gifts are made to several minor children or grandchildren each year.

If a gift is legitimate and outright, the annual gift-tax exclusion isn't lost merely because the named recipient is a minor. But a minor may have no legal capacity as to the subject matter of the gift, so it has to be made for her benefit—that is, to a trustee, guardian, or custodian. There is no gift if the donor has not actually relinquished the property. It isn't necessary that the property or its income actually be expended by or for the benefit of the minor during her period of minority, as long as all amounts not expended will pass to her when she reaches her 21st birthday. Should she die before that time, the property must be distributed to her estate or in accordance with her valid instructions on the subject.

Gifts to minors treated as present interests

Here are the ground rules. A transfer for the benefit of someone who hasn't reached age 21 on the date of the gift will qualify for the annual gift-tax exclusion (even though the property is beyond her grasp) if the conditions of the transfer meet all three of these requirements:

1. Property is transferred to a trust for the benefit of a minor and the trustee is given sole discretion, without substantial restriction, to decide whether or how to use the money on behalf of the minor. Both the property

itself and its income may be expended for the benefit of the donee before she reaches her 21st birthday, but it could be the donor's firm intention and expectation that no part of the gift will be touched before the minor reaches 21. In any case, it is not the minor who decides whether the gift may be expended by or for her. The phrase "may be expended" can refer to a mere grant of power to expend the trust funds or even to a probability that the funds will be used by or on behalf of the minor.

In one case, the court found that there was no substantial restriction on the trustee's discretion where he was authorized to spend trust money on the minor's behalf to cover costs and expenses "not otherwise adequately provided for." This kind of transaction, which comes out of the minor's need, is unlikely to be treated as a future interest ineligible for the annual exclusion. On the other hand, expenditures on the minor's behalf to be made only in the case of accident, illness, or other emergency would create restrictions on the trustee's discretion substantial enough to bar the annual exclusion.

2. Any portion of the property and its income not disposed of under (1) will pass to the child when she reaches age 21.

3. Any portion of the property and its income not disposed of under (1) will be payable either to the minor's estate or in accordance with other directions she has given in a will—for example, if she dies before reaching age 21. If, under state law, a minor does not have the legal right to make a will or otherwise dispose of property, the property will be distributed according to that state's laws of intestacy should she die before her 21st birthday. Customarily, the assets would then go to her next of kin, according to the state's definition of what that means.

A transfer will satisfy the above conditions even if:

a. The minor, upon reaching age 21, has the right to extend the terms of the trust.

b. The trust instrument contains provisions for disposition of the property in case the donee should die intestate.

Lower age for reaching majority in some states

Allowance of the annual exclusion is not affected in states that have lowered the age of majority from 21 to 18 and require property to be distributed to a donee when he/she reaches age 18.

You can't correct previous gifts

A trust agreement or other arrangement that does not include the three main requirements cannot be amended retroactively to obtain the annual gift-tax exclusion. Correction of a faulty document is impossible for federal tax purposes in this case, even where state law may permit it.

Conclusions and advice

• Start a program of gifts to your children or grandchildren as soon as possible in order to take maximum advantage of the annual exclusions. The fact that the minor is a very young child need not be a deterrent.

• You must let go of the property completely, even though the minor can't touch it.

• Use a trust or other separate entity for gifts to minors in order to show your complete divestiture. But if you use a trust, unearned income of a child under 14 is taxed at the parents' top tax rate in the case of transfers made after March 1, 1986.

- Do not make gifts to minors in the form of future interests.

- Do not count on getting back the property you have given to your minor child if she dies before reaching age 21. True, you may be next of kin. But the minor, unless of very tender years, might have taken steps that would frustrate this.

- Do not entrust your company's lawyer with the responsibility for setting up this arrangement. State law is involved in various respects, such as the age for attaining majority and what constitutes a gift. Use an attorney who is familiar with your state's laws.

- If parents establish a custodial account for their minor child, but she will have control over the funds when she reaches the state's age of legal maturity (usually 18), the account then in the minor's name will reduce the amount of college financial aid that might otherwise be available to her.

Chapter Eleven

THE UNIFORM GIFTS TO MINORS ACT

For many years the making of gifts to minors in the form of securities has presented a difficult practical problem. The act of gifting is simple enough, but what happens later if the minor chooses to sell the securities? A minor has the power to repudiate contracts or to disaffirm sales upon attaining majority, age 21 in most states but less in others. As a result, brokers, banks, or other parties are reluctant to buy securities from minors. Their reasoning: If the market value of the securities goes down after the sale, the minor could choose to let it stand. But if the market value rises, he/she might repudiate the sale upon reaching majority. The New York Stock Exchange, which is interested in the unhampered purchase and sale of securities, was largely responsible for passage of the Uniform Gifts to Minors Act, which, with some variations, has now been adopted by each of the states.

Ground rules for uniform gifts to minors

These laws eliminate the usual requirement that a trust be set up or a guardian be appointed when a minor is to be the donee of a gift. Instead, a custodian is named, who can be any adult. But the donor should not name himself as custodian, or the property will be included in his gross estate if he dies before the minor reaches 21. (One benefit of a custodianship: Setting it up is cheaper and simpler than setting up a trust.) Title to the gifted property rests absolutely with the minor. But the custodian has sole discretion to apply as much of the principal or income held by him for the benefit of the minor as he sees fit. Principal and income that are used are to be delivered to the donee when he reaches the legal age of majority, or, if he dies a minor, to his estate. But while he is still a minor, sales of securities may be made only by an adult custodian; the old practical problem of sales by a minor is therefore eliminated.

In the event of registered securities, delivery need not be made to the custodian, provided they are registered in his name followed by the words "as custodian for (name of minor) under the (name of enacting state) Uniform Gifts to Minors Act." In the case of unregistered securities, a donor must deliver them to the designated custodian with a statement of gift in the following form, signed by the donor and the custodian:

"Gift under the (name of enacting state) Uniform Gifts to Minors Act. I (name of donor) hereby deliver to (name of custodian) as custodian for (name of minor) under the (name of enacting state) Uniform Gifts to Minors Act, the following security(ies): (Insert a description of the security or securities delivered sufficient to identify it or them)."

Gift-tax treatment for securities—and other forms of gift

A transfer of securities to a minor under the Uniform Gifts to Minors Act constitutes a completed gift for federal tax purposes at the time the transfer is made. It qualifies for the annual gift exclusion of up to $10,000 per donee.

No taxable gift occurs for federal gift-tax purposes by reason of a subsequent resignation of the custodian or termination of the custodianship.

An adult may, during his lifetime, make a gift of a life insurance policy, an annuity contract, or money to someone who is a minor on the date of the gift.

If the gift is a life insurance policy or annuity contract, it can be made by having the ownership of the policy or contract registered with the issuing insurance company in the name of the custodian, followed by the words "as custodian for (name of minor) under the (name of enacting state) Uniform Gifts to Minors Act." If the gift is money, it is made by delivering it to a domestic financial institution or broker for credit to an account in the name of the custodian, followed by the words "as custodian for (name of minor) under the (name of enacting state) Uniform Gifts to Minors Act."

A donor who makes a gift to a minor in the manner described here must do everything possible to put the gift in the possession and control of the custodian. But neither the donor's failure to comply with the requirements nor his designation of an ineligible person (for example, another minor) as custodian, nor renunciation by the person designated as custodian, affects the completion of the gift. What could be affected is the donor's own tax liability if he has not properly parted with all interest in the property. In that case, the property may be includable in his own gross estate when he dies, for he has not effectively parted with the assets.

A transfer made under the Uniform Gifts to Minors Act is irrevocable.

Income-tax treatment

Income derived from property transferred under the Uniform Gifts to Minors Act is taxable to the minor donee. But to the extent that the income is used in the discharge or satisfaction of a legal obligation of any person to support or maintain a minor, it is taxable to that person. For example, a father has a legal obligation to support his minor child. If income earned by securities in a custodianship he created is used to provide support for the child, the father is taxed. See the discussion on the "kiddie tax" under Item 16 in Chapter Two, "Hidden Traps in Estate Planning."

Estate-tax treatment

The value of property transferred to a minor under the Uniform Gifts to Minors Act is includable in the gross estate of the donor for federal estate-tax purposes if he appoints himself custodian and dies while serving in that capacity and before the donee attains the age of majority. In all other circumstances, custodial property is includable only in the gross estate of the donee, the minor.

Successor custodian

Only an adult member of the minor's family, a guardian of the minor, or a trust company is, in general, eligible to become successor custodian. A custodian may designate his successor by executing and dating an instrument of designation before a witness other than the successor; this instrument of designation may but does not have to contain the successor's resignation. If he doesn't designate his successor in this manner before he dies and the minor has reached the age of 14, the minor may designate a successor custodian by executing an instrument of designation before a witness other than the successor.

Conclusions and advice

• You can remove property from what will become your gross estate by transferring it under the Uniform Gifts to Minors Act without that property being under the minor's control. As a result, potential buyers of the property won't be deterred by fears of repudiation of the transaction when the minor attains majority.

• You can use the Uniform Gifts to Minors Act for properties other than securities, for which the procedure was originally developed.

• There are differences in the various state laws enacted in accordance with the Uniform Gifts to Minors Act. Have a lawyer who is familiar with the legislation in your state check the form and language you intend to use.

• You do not have to set up a trust for the benefit of your minor child if a custodianship will accomplish the same result at considerable savings in cost and red tape.

• Do not name yourself or your spouse as custodian.

• Do not seek to revoke or repudiate a gift made under the Uniform Gifts to Minors Act. It can't be done.

Chapter Twelve

USE OF
NET GIFTS

A would-be donor who wants to give property away to beneficiaries might be deterred from making lifetime gifts because of the prospect of having to pay federal gift tax if the gift is in excess of the annual exclusion or if the unified gift- and estate-tax credit has already been used up. Or he may not want to exhaust the entire credit at this time, preferring to reserve some of it for the future. So he fails to make gifts for these reasons:

1. He may be unwilling to pay the gift tax at this time. He is likely to reason that he isn't going to be the one who pays the estate tax after he dies. His beneficiaries will pay in the sense that estate assets going to them will be decreased by the tax his estate must pay.

2. He may not be in a position to pay the gift tax despite his wealth. His assets could have appreciated mightily, but he is nevertheless cash-

poor because his wealth is tied up in his properties and it would be disadvantageous to liquidate them at this time.

3. Someone who has to sell assets in order to pay the gift tax is likely to have to pay income taxes on the sale of these assets, especially in inflationary times.

The advantage of net gifts

The edge of the donor's reluctance to pay gift taxes can be dulled through transfers of properties that can be spared to beneficiaries, subject to the condition that they pay the federal gift taxes. A gift conditional on the payment of federal gift tax by the donee is termed a net gift.

Here are the advantages of this procedure:

• The donor has reduced his ultimate gross estate.

• If the gift is of income-producing assets, he reduces his federal income taxes.

• He may save state and local property taxes, tangible and intangible, on property he no longer owns, as well as custody and insurance costs.

• The gift tax paid by the donee(s) is based on a lower figure than would be the case if the donor had paid the tax.

The net gift is computed by reducing the gross value of the gift by the amount of the tax the donee must pay in order to get it. The gift tax actually paid is based on that amount.

Will the donee(s) be willing to pay the federal gift tax as a condition of getting the property? Almost invariably, if the situation is explained to them. The donee may be anxious to get the property now instead of waiting until the death of the donor—and if an intended donee refuses to pay the gift tax, the property may never become his. The donor may feel impelled to dispose of it immediately, as in the case of real estate on which the carrying charges are greater than the current income, so he will select a more accommodating donee. Alternatively, the owner may decide to give the assets to an approved charitable organization, thus getting himself an income-tax deduction in the year of the contribution. If possibilities like these are suggested, the intended donee is indeed likely to agree to pay the gift tax.

When a donee is obliged to pay gift tax because of the conditions of the transfer, he may deduct the amount of the tax from the value of the gift subject to tax. This may require the use of an algebraic computation. The Internal Revenue Service can help with the computation, but the service should be asked for assistance well in advance of the date the return is due.

Proof that the gift was on a net basis

In order to achieve this favorable tax treatment—that is, payment of federal gift tax only on the difference between the value of the property and the amount of gift tax that would ordinarily be imposed—it must be clearly established that payment of the tax by the donee was an express condition of the transfer.

One transfer was considered to be a net gift in which the donees signed letters prepared by the donor's lawyer, stating: "We have further been informed that this gift is being made subject to my paying the gift tax on same. This letter can be taken as my acceptance of the proposed condition of the gift, and I agree to accept as my share of the gift tax an amount computed by your tax counsel."

This procedure may be used where an individual creates a trust for the benefit of someone else, such as his daughter. He transfers assets to the trust, subject to the condition that the trustee pay the federal gift tax. In one case, the trust instrument contained this language: "This gift is on the express condition that the Trustee report and pay out of the trust estate all gift taxes... imposed upon donor by virtue of this gift."

What may accompany gift-tax liability

A donee is responsible for the federal gift tax if the donor fails to pay it for any reason. If the donee has to pay the gift tax because the donor has failed to do so, any addition to the tax because of penalty imposed upon the donor for failure to file must be paid by the donee.

Income-tax consequences

It is a general principal of federal income taxation that when a solvent person is relieved of indebtedness, he has taxable income to that extent, for his financial condition has been improved. In the case of a net gift, the donor has made a transfer of property, but the donee, by paying the federal gift tax, directly or indirectly, has relieved the donor of paying this tax. If the recipient of a gift pays the federal gift tax that is by law imposed on the donor, the donor has income-tax liability to the extent of the discharge of his liability for gift tax. Inasmuch as this conclusion had not been reached by a court until March 4, 1981, no federal income tax is imposed upon persons who made net gifts (i.e., where the donee would pay the gift tax) prior to that date. The period of limitations for filing a claim for refund of tax thus overpaid is extended or reopened for up to one year after July 18, 1984.

Conclusions and advice:

- If you wish to take advantage of the net-gift treatment, have the donee agree in writing that he accepts this as a condition of the transfer.

- The donee must make certain that a federal gift-tax return is filed and any tax due gets paid. Otherwise he may lose the property in order to satisfy federal taxes found to be owing by the donor. If the transfer was not demonstrably a gift (and failure to file a gift-tax return suggests that it was not), the property may still be regarded as the donor's, subject to claims against him.

- Do not refuse a donor's gift conditioned upon your paying the gift tax without careful reflection. Your refusal could cost you the property.

- Do not assume that the donee is going to pay the tax; follow the matter up in order to ensure that this is done. A donee may be completely unaware of what he is to do, and the donor might be called upon to pay an unpaid tax resulting from his gift.

Chapter Thirteen

USING A CORPORATION TO TRANSFER ASSETS

We have discussed the desirability of a regular program of gift giving to intended beneficiaries. But most of an individual's properties will probably not be in the form of cash, which can be given away in any amount at any time. So if there are several beneficiaries, it won't be possible to give each one the desired undivided fractional interest in a piece of real estate, a going business, or a valuable collection of some sort. Nor is it likely that beneficiaries receiving undivided fractional interests in property of this kind will be able to handle them properly. Each might have his/her own idea of how the property should be managed, whether it should be sold, for how much and when, and the like. A prospective buyer of the property would be reluctant to negotiate with a variety of co-owners who might have different objectives.

A solution to this common problem is to give each beneficiary the proportion of the property you have selected for him/her while keeping actual ownership and management of the property in the hands of a responsible manager. This should not be you; for if you haven't really let go of the property, its value will be includable in your estate when you die.

Nonfragmented transfers

The plan: Transfer selected properties to a newly formed corporation in return for its stock. Then you can give or bequeath to each beneficiary the desired number of shares, at one time or over a period of years, in order to take advantage of the annual gift-tax exclusions. Here are the advantages:

1. Property can be given away currently even though it is not possible or feasible to fragmentize these assets.

2. Property can be given away in whatever amounts are desirable each year, such as $10,000 or $20,000 per donee, or any other figure. Instead of transferring to a particular beneficiary, say, a one-seventh interest in a piece of land, he/she can be given whatever number of corporate shares your accountant computes is worth $20,000 or whatever figure is desired.

3. A beneficiary need not fear that his/her interest in property will be of lessened value because of a co-owner's irresponsible behavior. The corporation should have as its executive a person of judgment and capacity. He/she will make the decisions, subject to ratification when required by a majority of the shareholders.

4. In the marketplace, the whole is customarily worth more than the sum of the parts. A beneficiary who owns an undivided fractional interest in property possesses a part. The corporation possesses the whole.

Tax-free transfer to corporation

Ordinarily if an individual owns property that has appreciated in value, he has a taxable gain when he disposes of it, such as by sale or exchange. But he can avoid present recognition of taxable gain on the transfer of his property to a corporation solely in return for its stock if, immediately after the transfer, he owns at least 80 percent of the stock. For the present purpose, it would be advisable that he receive all of the stock. He still owns the property at this point, although the form of ownership has been changed from direct to indirect. That is, he owns the stock of the corporation that owns the property.

If a husband and wife, or any other plural parties, transfer assets to a corporation in return for all of its stock, this is a transfer to a corporation that is collectively controlled by the transferors immediately after the transaction and is tax-free. But the Internal Revenue Service has the power to investigate whether there is any collectible tax if the stock the transferors receive is not substantially in proportion to the value of the properties transferred. For example, a father and son individually transfer assets to a corporation, each receiving 50 percent of the stock. But if the property the father transferred was worth more than twice the property the son transferred, the IRS may query why the father didn't receive two-thirds of the stock. Gift tax could be imposed on the ground that the father in effect got 66⅔ percent of the stock since he provided 66⅔ percent of the property and then gave the son 16⅔ percent—as a taxable gift—so that father and son each ended up with 50 percent of the stock.

The person transferring stock to a controlled corporation must receive corporate stock in return for it. The tax law does not disqualify tax-free treatment where property transferred to a controlled corporation isn't solely for stock. But if the individual transferring the property to the corporation receives not only its stock but any other property, he has a taxable gain in an amount not in excess of the fair market value of the other property he receives.

Income-tax consequences

Even though a person's transfer of property to a controlled corporation can be structured on a tax-free basis, there could be income-tax consequences for him. For example, he may transfer an office building to the corporation in return for its stock. The building carries a mortgage substantially in excess of his cost basis. To the extent that the mortgage debt transferred to the corporation exceeds his tax cost of the assets, he has taxable gain because he has been relieved of liabilities higher than the amount of assets disposed of. His financial position was improved by this amount.

Release from personal liability is the equivalent of taxable gain. It doesn't matter for this purpose whether this individual transferred to the corporation property subject to a liability in excess of his basis or whether the corporation assumed his liabilities. However, the tax law does not treat the assumption of ordinary trade payables as triggering income to the extent that such payables would be deductible by the transferor.

The property transferred to the controlled corporation has the same tax basis in the corporation's hands that it had in the individual's hands. If the property consists of capital assets, the length of time the individual owned them and the time the corporation later owns them are added together to establish whether the gain or loss resulting from subsequent sale by the corporation is long- or short-term.

Conclusions and advice

• Have restrictions as to transferability stamped upon stock certificates given to the beneficiaries so that they don't part with property that may be worth far more if outsiders aren't brought into the picture.

• A transfer to a controlled corporation is tax-free only where the transferor or transferors collectively own at least 80 percent of the stock immediately after the transfer. So they should not have any legal obligation to dispose of any of the shares at the time of the transfer. A "gentleman's agreement" to dispose of stock is acceptable.

• Do not select assets subject to liabilities in excess of the fair market value of what is transferred in transferring property to a controlled corporation.

Chapter Fourteen

THE MARITAL DEDUCTION: MAXIMIZING THE OPPORTUNITY

The marital deduction is a most significant factor in reducing the size of an estate for federal estate-tax purposes. The deduction permits an individual to pass on to his/her surviving spouse 100 percent of his adjusted gross estate free of estate tax. But now that very substantial portions of each estate may pass free of estate tax under the expanded unified credit, estate planners must consider the overall impact of taxes on both estates in deciding how much marital deduction to claim in the estate of the first spouse to die.

Each spouse can leave up to $600,000 free of estate tax. If all property goes to the surviving spouse, the credit applicable to the estate of the first spouse to die could be completely lost. The amount passing tax-free includes both lifetime and death-time transfers that would otherwise be taxable. (See also page 81.)

Money and other property passing from a decedent to a surviving spouse may qualify for the marital deduction even if they are in the form of a terminable interest, provided the interest is a qualified terminable interest. Executors now have added responsibility, as well as flexibility, in that they must decide whether or not to take the marital deduction for all or a portion of the qualified terminable interest.

What is meant by property passing to a surviving spouse

Property passing to the surviving spouse qualifies for the marital deduction. The definition of "passing" includes:

1. Property left by will.

2. Property acquired under state laws of intestacy when the decedent has not left a valid will. For example, state law might provide that a decedent's property go to the next of kin. In this case at least a portion of it would go to the surviving spouse.

3. Property going to the surviving spouse despite the language of a valid will, because the widow "took against the will" by claiming that part of her husband's estate to which she was entitled as dower. The husband may have a comparable right.

4. Property going to the widow as co-owner of the property with right of survivorship.

5. Insurance proceeds received by the surviving spouse under a policy on the life of the decedent.

6. Property that had been transferred to the surviving spouse.

7. Property that the decedent had the right to transfer under the authorization of a third party, if the decedent named the spouse as recipient.

8. Property in which the surviving spouse has a qualifying income interest, if the donor or the executor irrevocably elects to claim the marital deduction for the underlying qualified terminable interest property. For the rules that apply here, see Chapter Fifteen, "Where the Surviving Spouse Can't Touch Anything But Income."

The property passing to the surviving spouse means only what she actually receives, not what the will states she should receive.

Sometimes a disappointed heir threatens to contest a decedent's will. If, to settle the controversy, the surviving spouse agrees that a part of what the will states is to go to her should instead be paid directly to the claimant, the amount of property passing to her from the decedent is reduced accordingly.

Nonqualified terminable interests aren't deductible

A common form of nonqualifying terminable interest is a residence owned by the husband. His will provides that his wife is to have the right to reside in the house for as long as she lives; then the property is to go to the children. Her interest in the property that passes to her from her husband is a nonqualifying terminable interest, for she can't will the house to anyone of her choice, and she has no right to income payable at least annually.

If property is left to a spouse subject to a contingency, there is a nonqualifying terminable interest, even if that contingency doesn't occur.

One man's will left his property to his wife "to have and to hold absolutely." But in a later paragraph, the will stated that if she remarried, the property was to go to their children. Because the property passing to the wife was subject to this condition, it was not eligible for the marital deduction. And because the property was not certain to be included in the wife's estate, it could not be a qualified terminable interest.

The right to sell—but not to give

Another man left all his real estate to his wife for life, giving her the right to sell any or all of it as she saw fit. The will then provided that any of the real estate that the wife still owned when she died was to go to the children. The realty interest left to her obviously couldn't qualify for the marital deduction—she did not have a complete interest in the property. Although she could sell it, the will did not empower her to give it away. Perhaps the power to give the property away was omitted from the will through carelessness. At any rate, the deduction was lost.

But if the decedent's will merely contains words like "it is my wish and desire" that any of the property his widow holds at the time of her death go to the children, the property passing to her will qualify for the marital deduction. She receives the property unconditionally. It is likely that she would honor her husband's request, but the choice is hers alone.

Another man's will provided his wife with a life—or terminable—interest in a trust. This did not qualify for the marital deduction under the law then in effect. But in a codicil, or supplementary addition to the will, he provided that she could substitute for the interest in the trust a stated amount of cash—to be paid outright—if she so advised the executor within

60 days of her husband's death. That is what she did, and the cash she received represented an absolute right to a nonterminable interest, thus qualifying for the marital deduction. (Presumably, in this case, an alert estate planner, reviewing his/her client's plans, spotted the language that would have forfeited the marital deduction and was able to correct it in time.)

Situations like these led the United States Supreme Court to declare, "The achievement of the purpose of the marital deduction is dependent to a great degree upon the careful drafting of wills." The language of the will, not the good intentions of the testator or the lawyers, determines the qualification for the marital deduction.

Disclaimers

If the surviving spouse makes a disclaimer of any property interest that would otherwise be considered as having passed to her from the decedent, the disclaimed interest is considered as having passed directly to the person entitled to receive the interest as a result of this disclaimer. Thus, the disclaimed interest is not entitled to the benefit of the marital deduction. (See Chapter Thirty-seven, "Disclaimers and Renunciations.")

Effects of state law

The question of the marital deduction for federal estate-tax purposes may be subject to state law. If a marriage has not been recognized by the state in which the spouses resided at the time of death of one of them, there can be no marital deduction. Further, any interest passing to the surviving spouse must be valid under the property laws of the state in which it was created.

Bequests to noncitizen spouse

The estate-tax marital deduction is allowed for property passing to a noncitizen spouse if the spouse becomes a US citizen before the estate-tax return is filed, provided the spouse was a US resident at the date of the decedent's death and at all times before becoming a US citizen. In addition, all property, probate and nonprobate, passing to a noncitizen qualifies for the marital deduction if the property is transferred or irrevocably assigned to a qualifying domestic trust (QDT) before the estate-tax return is filed. (There is no requirement that this trust be created by the decedent. It may be created by the executor or the surviving spouse.) Property passing from decedents who died before December 19, 1989, is treated as qualifying for the marital deduction if transferred or assigned to a QDT within one year of that date. Property passing from a nonresident, noncitizen to a noncitizen spouse qualifies for the estate-tax marital deduction if it passes in a QDT.

Second-to-die (or survivorship) insurance

When an estate plan calls for the use of the unlimited marital deduction, no federal estate tax is paid by the estate of the first spouse to die (here called the husband solely for convenience) upon the value of property passing to the survivor under the conditions mentioned in this chapter. But when the second spouse (here called the wife) dies, there is a pyramid amount of property to be taxed: her own property plus what she had received, courtesy of the unlimited marital deduction, from her husband's estate. Now there is a larger amount of estate tax to be paid than would be the case if her husband's estate had paid the tax on the value of the property passing to her upon his death.

The solution: survivorship insurance. Under this policy, the insurance company pays out nothing on the property passing under the marital deduction when the husband dies. When the wife subsequently dies, the executor or heirs receive from the insurance company an amount that had been calculated to pay the estate tax upon her own estate plus what she had received under the unlimited marital deduction.

The cost of such a policy is far less than the cost of insuring each spouse separately because the insurance company must pay out—at some future time—only one amount.

Inasmuch as the estate of the second spouse to die must pay the tax nine months after her death, this arrangement can avoid a sale of estate assets at what could be just the wrong time in order to raise the enhanced tax. Funds provided by this type of insurance can avoid the hasty sale of assets.

Sometimes the marital deduction isn't desired

There are occasions when an individual doesn't want to leave a surviving spouse any amount that would qualify for the marital deduction. If, for example, a spouse has ample wealth of her own, the testator might elect to provide for other people, or for institutions. Or the survivor might be very ill, or elderly.

Conclusions and advice

• In cases of prior marriage and divorce, be sure your present marriage is recognized as valid under state law.

• Consider leaving a surviving spouse qualified terminable interest property to provide the executor with flexibility in reducing taxes in both spouses' estates.

- Do not use conflicting language in the will that could forfeit the marital deduction. The language should be reviewed by someone who is familiar with federal estate-tax law.

- You may better serve your estate-planning objectives by deliberately bypassing the marital deduction.

- The marital deduction is not available for property passing to an alien spouse. Gifts to an alien spouse exceeding $100,000 a year are taxable under the federal gift tax. The estate-tax marital deduction is allowed for property passing to an alien spouse in a qualified domestic trust. Property passing outside the probate estate is treated as passing in a qualified domestic trust if it is transferred to the trust before the estate-tax return is due. A qualified domestic trust must meet four specified conditions.

- See "credit equivalent trusts" on Page 22.

Chapter Fifteen

WHERE THE SURVIVING SPOUSE CAN'T TOUCH ANYTHING BUT INCOME

The idea of transferring a complete interest in a substantial part of his wealth to his surviving spouse has disturbed many a thoughtful husband in planning the disposition of his estate. Perhaps the spouse is too financially unsophisticated to be given control over property that may be intended to provide her with support and comfort for the remainder of her life. Perhaps she doesn't want the responsibilities and chores involved in property ownership and management. Maybe the husband believes that if his widow has been left too tempting a sum outright, she will be prey to fortune hunters. The obvious answer would be to give her merely a life interest in income, without the headaches and nuisances of property ownership. As of 1982, the husband has been able to do just that, provided the interest is a qualifying life interest in qualified terminable interest property (referred to by the acronym

"Q-tip property"), and he or his executor elect irrevocably to claim the marital deduction for all or a portion of such property. The election to treat property as if no Q-tip election had been made must be made with respect to all the property in the Q-tip trust. For example, if a spouse makes a Q-tip election with respect to $1,400,000 of a $2,000,000 trust, he must elect to claim the marital deduction with respect to the entire $1,400,000 in order to make the generation-skipping election.

Qualified terminable interest property provides an elective deduction

The executor may elect to claim the marital deduction for qualified terminable interest property. Such property may or may not be an interest in a trust. Very frequently, however, a trust is used to achieve the desired result. The surviving spouse must have a qualified life interest in the property, which means that income from the property must be paid to her at least annually. If there is a trust, the trustee may have the discretionary right to use the principal for the surviving spouse's benefit. But neither he, the spouse, nor anyone else may have the power to appoint the property itself to anyone during the spouse's lifetime. At her death, however, such powers may be exercised.

Under a properly established Q-tip trust, a life interest granted to a surviving spouse is not automatically treated as an ordinary terminable interest that is taxable to the estate of the decedent. Rather, the estate is permitted to make a Q-tip election to defer the payment of estate taxes. If the estate so elects, the Q-tip trust property is then treated as passing outright from the decedent to the surviving spouse. Because such treatment brings the trust property within the confines of the unlimited marital deduction, the property is not taxed in the decedent's estate. It is taxed later, however, as part of the surviving spouse's estate.

Where the Q-tip requirements are met, the entire proceeds (a life income interest and the remainder of the underlying Q-tip property) is treated as passing to the surviving spouse and qualifies for the marital deduction. To the extent that it is not consumed or disposed of during the surviving spouse's life, the value of the entire property is included in the gross estate of the surviving spouse.

A Q-tip may be created by a lifetime gift as well as at death. If so created, the donor makes the election to have the interest qualify for the marital deduction.

If Q-tip property qualifies for the marital deduction, it must be subject to tax in the estate of the second spouse to die. To make sure such taxation occurs, the law precipitates tax on the underlying property if the surviving spouse gives away her income interest. At that point, the unified-transfer tax on the property itself becomes due.

The Q-tip device provides a new and very flexible device for minimizing taxes on both estates. If a Q-tip interest is present, the executor can elect to claim the marital deduction for only that portion of the property that exceeds the amount of property subject to the credit. Since much property may pass to the surviving spouse outside the will—such as jointly owned property, insurance, or employee-plan benefits—the executor can take into account all such property when making his election.

The transfer to a spouse of an interest in a joint and survivor annuity in which only the spouse has the right to receive any payments prior to the death of the last spouse to die qualifies for a marital deduction under the

Q-tip rules. Such transfer, however, does not qualify if either the donor or the executor, as the case may be, irrevocably elects out of Q-tip treatment.

A joint and survivor annuity is treated as qualifying under the Q-tip rule only if the annuity is includable in the decedent's estate as an annuity. Thus, an annuity created by the decedent's will does not qualify.

The new Q-tip interests must be created with great care to make sure they are in perfect agreement with the requirements and regulations of the law. This places a new burden on the executor and makes it more important than ever that he/she be chosen with care.

This new device does not mean that the older-type marital deduction trust, where the wife received not only the income interest but also the right to decide who would receive the principal after her death, won't continue to be effective. If properly drawn, such a trust will still qualify for the marital deduction, but it lacks the flexibility that allows an executor to decide whether, and how much of, the trust should get the marital deduction.

There are some reasons why the Q-tip election may seem unattractive. Your executor may not be familiar with the procedure. If he/she makes the election, it cannot subsequently be revoked. The surviving spouse may in effect cancel the executor's election. The amount of property she consumes will affect the amount that is left after she dies. In short, an individual who is planning his estate has no assurance that the property will be distributed in line with what he has in mind. He is therefore surrendering some of his options.

In addition, it may be easier to finance two partial estate taxes (on the death of the husband and, perhaps much later, upon the death of the surviving spouse) than to pay what may be a far higher tax on the second death, when the survivor's property plus the unconsumed portion of the husband's also may be taxable. The tax rates that would be in effect when the second spouse dies are unpredictable. So are values of the property that had belonged to the husband. But additional time has been purchased to decide what disposition is to be made of the husband's property.

An individual considering the use of the Q-tip alternative would be well advised to consult a competent professional adviser, as the controlling tax laws have been changed several times in the past few years.

Couple a life interest with dispositive powers

A plan may be made, however, that will give the surviving spouse merely a life income, without the possibility of wasting or losing the principal that produces this income; this would free her from the duties of property administration. But the interest transferred to her can still participate in the benefit of the marital deduction.

The ground rules

The marital deduction is not lost when a surviving spouse is given a life interest in income from a trust that meets the following conditions:

1. The surviving spouse must be entitled for life to all of the income from the entire interest, or to all of the income from a specific portion of this interest. The "specific portion" now means a portion determined on a fractional or percentage basis; in the case of decedents dying after October 24, 1992, it no longer includes a specified or fixed dollar amount..

2. The income must be payable annually or at more frequent intervals. It must be distributed currently to the surviving spouse or practically it must be virtually hers. The governing instrument of one trust provided for

the income each year to be paid quarterly during the following years: In that case, the marital deduction was forfeited. Because there was a mandatory delay of at least a year before income could be paid out, payment of income was not considered current.

3. The surviving spouse must have a power of appointment over the principal of the entire interest or a specific portion. A "power of appointment," for this purpose, means the right to control the ultimate disposition of designated property, the trust principal remaining when the surviving spouse dies. (See Chapter Thirty-six, "Powers of Appointment.") The crucial point here is that the surviving spouse must have the right to name in her will the person who will get the trust property after her death, without in any way being restricted by conditions imposed by her late husband when he transferred the property to the trust. In order for the property passing under the husband's will to qualify for the marital deduction, the power of appointment must be in existence at the time the property itself passes. This means that it must be absolute and unconditional.

4. In effect, no other person can have the power to appoint any part of the interest to any person other than the surviving spouse.

5. This also means that power must be exercisable by the surviving spouse alone and in all events. One decedent's will gave his wife the right to dispose of the property as she saw fit. But she was incompetent and was therefore unable to enter into a legal transaction without the intervention of a guardian. Accordingly, her power of appointment over the property was not exercisable "alone and in all events," and the marital deduction wasn't allowed to the husband's estate.

With respect to persons dying after December 31, 1983, no marital deduction is allowed for any claim against a surviving spouse's estate for an interest for which a Q-tip property election was made by the first spouse to die.

Surviving spouse can't be under restraints

In one case, the decedent provided that his wife would receive the trust income for life, with a right to stipulate in her will who would get any remaining trust principal. But he further provided that if she made any attempt to assign her right to the trust income, her absolute right to the trust income would cease and the trustee would then provide her with whatever income was, in the trustee's sole discretion, necessary for her support. This was done to protect the trust from any effort by the wife or their sole discretion, to pay a portion of the principal to her for support of the husband's descendants. His estate was entitled to the marital deduction. The trustee could use principal only if he agreed to her "requests," which she was not required to make. Since principal could be diverted to others during the wife's lifetime only by her initiative, this power did not curtail the right given to her by her husband's will to designate the recipients of any remaining amount of principal when she died.

Faulty wording can be fatal

The will of one individual, after certain bequests, left the remainder of his property in trust for the benefit of his wife. The trust instrument provided that she was entitled to support and maintenance for life, not to "all of the income" from the residue of the estate. Nor was it specified that she would be entitled to the income "annually or at more frequent intervals." This careless draftsmanship of the will resulted in forfeiture of the marital deduction.

90

Impact of state law

In some states, a widow is not permitted to designate her own estate or her creditors as parties who can receive the trust principal. As a result, she does not have the power to determine who is to get the principal in all instances and the estate does not qualify for the marital deduction.

Conclusions and advice

- To qualify for the marital deduction without placing property at the disposition of a surviving spouse who may not have the ability or desire to care for it, provide for a qualified terminable interest in your will. This new device will give your executor flexibility in deciding what portion of this interest should qualify for the marital deduction and what portion should be included in your taxable estate.

- Remember that a trust providing your spouse with a life income and the right to dispose of the remaining principal will qualify for the marital deduction.

- Do not attempt to qualify life income for the marital deduction without getting advice from experienced counsel on the technical ground rules.

- Remember that you should consider the total tax bill payable by your estate and your spouse's. It is important that each of you get the full benefit of the unified-estate- and gift-tax credit.

- The marital deduction can apply to gift tax as well as estate tax.

Chapter Sixteen

JOINT AND MUTUAL WILLS

A husband may desire to leave all of his property, or a substantial portion of it, to his spouse. But he fears that if his will so provides, and he is the one to die first, upon her death any of his remaining property will be left by her to her own relatives, friends, and favorite charitable organizations. So that his sister, children by a prior marriage, and university are not forgotten, he bequeathes his wife only a limited portion of his wealth and makes disposition of the remainder to his own nominees. For her part, the wife may have comparable reluctance to will most or all of her property to her husband, because doing so could mean that should she die first, her side of the family and her interests might not be provided for in his will. Even if his will did make such provisions, it's possible that he would revise that testament after she dies. As a result, neither spouse provides by will for the other as much as they would like to provide or receive.

Joint (or mutual) wills

A practical solution to this common problem may take either of two related forms: the joint will or mutual wills.

A joint will, which is signed by both spouses, customarily provides that on the death of one of them, all of his or her property, or a designated substantial portion of it, will go to the survivor. On the death of the second spouse, that party's property (including what remains of the first spouse's wealth) will pass to specified relatives, friends, and chosen charitable organizations of each spouse in amounts or in proportions that were agreed to when the will was prepared.

The main advantage of the joint will is that in it both spouses can make generous, perhaps total, provision for the survivor, with the assurance that their own relatives, friends, and charities will not be bypassed upon the death of the second spouse. The main disadvantage in most circumstances is loss of the marital deduction from the estate tax, which is available in the case of property that goes to the surviving spouse. The marital deduction isn't available in joint wills because what the surviving spouse receives is not an outright transfer to do with as she/he sees fit, which is a requirement for the marital deduction, because neither spouse has the right to dispose of this property according to his or her own wishes when they both die. He/she receives the property subject to a preexisting formula of disposition. (See Chapter Fourteen, "The Marital Deduction.")

Approved wording for use in a joint will

Here is an example of language used in a very simple form of joint will, quoted by the court in one case:

"After the death of either of us, and after the payment of our funeral expenses and just debts, we give, devise, and bequeath all the balance of our estate...of whatsoever kind and nature and wheresoever situated that either shall die seized and possessed of, to whomsoever shall be the survivor of us....At the time of the death of the survivor of us, or if we should both die at the same time, if there be anything left, then we give, devise and bequeath to our children, Raymond D. Dekker and Lillian Laughlin, all of our property...share and share alike."

A joint will can be very complex where detailed provision is made for ultimate specific bequests or proportions of the estate to various relatives, friends, and favorite charitable organizations of each spouse.

Approved wording for use in mutual wills

Mutual wills are separate testaments by each spouse, prepared after they have worked out an understanding and agreement as to how property dispositions at death will be made. One spouse in effect is agreeing to leave certain amounts or proportions of his property in a specified manner in return for the other spouse's agreement as to how she will leave her property.

Here is the language of a wife's mutual will quoted by a court in one decision:

"In consideration of the mutual will on this date executed by my husband, W. D. Newman, I give, devise, and bequeath to my husband, W. D. Newman, all of my property, both real and personal, and all effects of every kind and nature whatsoever and wheresoever situated, of which I may die seized and possessed, or to which I may be entitled at the time of my decease, to have and to hold same as an absolute estate forever. This will is a mutual will executed contemporaneously with the aforesaid mutual will of my husband, W. D. Newman, and each is consideration for the other, and the provisions of same are reciprocal, and it is the express intention and desire, based upon said consideration, that each of our respective wills be irrevocable....

"In the event my husband shall be deceased at the time of my decease, then I give, devise, and bequeath all of my property...to my children, Arthur Newman, Mildred Jones, and William D. Newman, Jr., in equal shares, share and share alike; and in the event that any of my said children predecease me leaving a child or children surviving, I direct that such child or children of my deceased child shall take per stirpes the parent's share, and in the event any of my said children shall be deceased at the time of my death leaving no child or children surviving, then I direct that the share of my said deceased child shall be divided among my children surviving me or their child or children surviving, who shall take per stirpes the parent's share."

The husband's will was similar in all of its provisions, except that where the wife's will left everything to the husband, his will left everything to her.

Mutual wills, too, can be very complex, especially in cases where only a specified amount or proportion of each spouse's property will go to the survivor, or where there is a detailed scenario as to how property remaining at the death of the second spouse is to be apportioned among various beneficiaries.

A husband and wife jointly signed a will providing that if they died simultaneously or so closely together that the survivor did not have time to probate the will, properties would go to beneficiaries designated in this document. Any property not so disposed of would go to the children in equal amounts. The marital deduction applies to this situation, says the Internal Revenue Service (Technical Advice Memoranda 8523004, February 22, 1985).

Approved wording for use in consent to other spouse's will

One spouse may, by a separate document, consent to be bound by the terms of the other's will in the case of property dispositions and other arrangements. Here is an example of the language of one such agreement quoted in court:

"I, EMMA BRESSANI, wife of RICHARD V. BRESSANI, also known as RICHARD VALENTINE BRESSANI, the maker of the foregoing Will, having read it in its entirety, and clearly understanding that my said husband by his said Will disposes not only of his separate estate, in case there be any such, but also all of our community property, including the share thereof which I would be entitled to take and receive by law upon his death, as well as his own share or interest therein, and being fully convinced in my own mind of the reasonableness and equity of said Will and the wisdom of its provisions, and in consideration of the provisions made for me therein, hereby elect to and do accept, acquiesce in, and consent to said Will and all of its provisions, including disposition at the death of my said husband and [sic] all of our community property. I hereby accept such of the said provisions of said Will as apply to or concern me."

Danger of mutual wills

The possible weakness of mutual wills is that after property dispositions are agreed to by both spouses and the wills are reviewed by lawyers of both, one spouse subsequently may write a new will, the first paragraph of which specifically cancels any previous will. The consequence is that the wife, let us assume, has made dispositions in return for reciprocal commitments by her husband which he, without her awareness, has later canceled. State laws and court decisions vary as to whether a mutual will creates a legal obligation or merely a moral one.

Under the laws of some states, the child of a party to mutual wills cannot be deprived of his/her rights if one spouse's will is replaced by a later version.

Common disasters

Joint and mutual wills should make provision for the property dispositions to be made if both parties die simultaneously or when it is not possible to determine the order of dying in a common disaster. (See Chapter Seventeen, "Simultaneous Deaths of Spouses.")

Conclusions and advice

- Realize that the use of joint or mutual wills forfeits the marital deduction. Balance the consequences before making your choice.

• Inasmuch as state laws vary as to the effect of making joint and mutual wills, and simultaneous deaths of spouses, have the wills checked by an attorney who is familiar with the particular laws of your state. In some states a beneficiary is not an acceptable witness. In others, the will must be handwritten.

• Provide for what is to happen in the case of the simultaneous deaths of both spouses. If state law made disposition of a husband's property where his wife survived him by fewer than a specified number of hours, a detailed survivorship clause in the husband's will had precedence over the state law.

• Do not use joint or mutual wills if there is any likelihood of a divorce.

• Do not take it for granted that a mutual will shall not be repudiated by your spouse.

• The parties may make living wills, which can state their wishes about life-sustaining treatment. Specific statements can be made about desired medical procedures such as cardiopulmonary resuscitation, artificial measures of nutrition, kidney dialysis, artificial respiration, surgery, and medicines.

Chapter Seventeen

SIMULTANEOUS DEATHS OF SPOUSES

There is a tendency to assume that one spouse, most frequently the party whose estate is being planned, will die before the other does. But it is wise to have contingency plans in case both spouses die in a common disaster, where it isn't possible to determine the sequence of their deaths. The order of their deaths is significant in such areas as the distribution of jointly owned property, life insurance, the marital deduction, and powers of appointment.

Uniform-simultaneous-death legislation

It is state and not federal law that covers the sequence of deaths in a common disaster where there is not sufficient evidence that the parties died otherwise than simultaneously. Most states have adopted some version of the Uniform Simultaneous Deaths Act. The purpose of this legislation is to solve the problem of the passage of property when distribution depends upon the order of death and the circumstances are such that it is not ascertainable.

Joint ownership of property

In a state that has adopted the Uniform Simultaneous Deaths Act, where there isn't sufficient evidence that two joint owners of property or tenants by the entirety have died other than simultaneously, the property so held is to be distributed one-half as if one had survived and one-half as if the other had survived. Ordinarily in a joint tenancy, upon the death of one owner, all of the property goes to the survivor(s). In the case of a tenancy by the entirety, which can be used only by legally married couples, the entire property goes to the survivor. (See Chapter Eighteen, "Choice of Forms of Ownership.")

For federal estate-tax purposes, where property is held in a tenancy by the entirety at the time of, say, the husband's death, one-half the value of the property will be includable in the husband's gross estate. The other one-half will be part of the wife's estate. This is in accord with the Uniform Simultaneous Deaths Act.

Life insurance

Where there is a policy of insurance upon the life of one person, payable upon his/her death to a named beneficiary, under the Uniform Simultaneous Deaths Act the insured will be presumed to have survived the beneficiary. So it is advisable for a contingent beneficiary to be named so that the proceeds would go to a specifically selected person should both the insured and the beneficiary die in a common disaster.

A wife owned insurance policies upon the life of her husband. They were killed simultaneously in an airplane crash, and the Internal Revenue Service sought to include the policy proceeds in her gross estate. But under the Uniform Simultaneous Deaths Act, at the moment of her death the proceeds of the policies on his life had not yet matured by reason of his death, so only the value of the policies at that moment, and not the death benefits, was includable in her estate.

The marital deduction

In those states where the Uniform Simultaneous Deaths Act is in force, and it is impossible to determine the sequence of death of husband and wife, the estate is not entitled to the marital deduction since no property could have passed from one to the other.

Except for qualified terminable interest property, no marital deduction is available in cases where the interest passing to a surviving spouse is a terminable one. (See Chapter Fourteen, "The Marital Deduction.") But if the testator specifies that the only conditions under which passage of property to the survivor would be terminated under the will are (a) a common disaster under which both spouses die, or (b) death of the surviving spouse within six months of the testator's death, and neither of these conditions occurs, the marital deduction is preserved.

Reverse-simultaneous-death clause

A will may provide that in the case of a common disaster, the person who wrote the will shall be deemed to have died first. The wills of both husband and wife can contain such a provision. Then the property going to the spouse surviving under this created presumption will qualify for the marital deduction. This is usually advisable when one spouse—usually the husband—is much wealthier than the other.

Another instance in which such a clause is desirable: When the wife is the wealthier party and the husband wants his property to go to his children by a prior marriage or to other relatives.

Power of appointment

The gross estate may include a power of appointment created by will where the party to whom the power was granted, the holder, died prior to the probating of the will that created the power. This may come about where the creator of the power and the holder die in a simultaneous accident. If, under state law, the holder's power of appointment becomes effective immediately and is not postponed until probate or until any other time later than the death of the creator of the power, the holder possessed the power at the time of her death, and the property subject to it is includable in her gross estate, even though, as a practical matter, she never had an opportunity to do anything about it because of the common disaster.

Will provisions

Consider making a provision that if the deaths of the spouses occur in a common disaster, each spouse will leave to their now-orphaned children what would otherwise have gone to the surviving spouse.

A will or other form of property disposition may provide for two or more beneficiaries in a designated manner of succession. For example, property may be bequeathed to an individual's son and daughter, with the provision that if these beneficiaries should not survive the testator, their shares will pass to the testator's grandchildren; the amount each grandchild receives would be a proportion of what the original beneficiaries would have gotten. The Uniform Simultaneous Deaths Act provides that where two or more beneficiaries are named to inherit successively by reason of survivorship under another person's disposition of property, and there is not sufficient evidence that these beneficiaries died otherwise than simultaneously, the property thus disposed of will be divided into as many equal portions as there are successive beneficiaries. These portions would then be distributed respectively to those who would have inherited in the event that each designated beneficiary had survived.

Conclusions and advice

• Have local counsel check the simultaneous-death law of the particular state in which you live, as state law may govern the federal tax treatment. If you move to another state, have local counsel there restudy your situation.

• Name contingent beneficiaries in the event of simultaneous deaths of spouses.

• Check carefully to see whether you are willing to have the Uniform Simultaneous Deaths Act apply. If not, adopt a reverse-simultaneous-death clause in the will. This decision should be reviewed periodically in the light of changing circumstances.

• Do not assume that spouses will die at different times, despite major differences in age or state of health.

• Do not assume that the Uniform Simultaneous Deaths Act is confined to spouses. For example, it applies to unrelated joint owners of property as well.

• Do not take for granted that if the spouses die in a common disaster, the simultaneous death laws will apply. Even if the parties die in the same accident, there may be evidence that one died before the other.

Chapter Eighteen

CHOICE OF FORMS OF OWNERSHIP

The manner in which property is owned is most meaningful for estate-planning purposes. It affects the passage of property when an owner dies; it may insulate part of the value from creditor claims; and there are federal estate, gift, and income tax implications.

At the time of a person's death, the value of all the property he owns is included in his gross estate. If his interest in a property is actually and demonstrably less than 100 percent, only the applicable portion of its value will be included in his estate. So joint ownership can reduce the amount of the estate tax.

Why property may be held in joint ownership

There are various justifications for owning property with someone else:

1. Fait accompli: Property may have been acquired by two or more persons, so that form of ownership represents the fact. Examples: Each of the purchasers of an asset supplied some of the funds. Or the property was acquired jointly by gift, as when a bride and groom are given a house or securities by one set of parents.

2. Protection: An individual wishes to make certain that upon his death the property will go to designated parties without danger that someone else may claim the assets. A husband may wish the residence to go to his wife, without interference from the children. Or a mother may set up a joint bank account with her daughter so that the money in this account will unquestionably be the daughter's even if sons claim a portion after the mother's death.

3. Avoidance of probate: Joint ownership of property with a survivorship provision will avoid the delay, expense, and publicity involved in probate. Under a survivorship provision, upon the death of a co-owner, his/her interest automatically passes to the survivor(s). The dispositions of a will are open to an inquisitive public when the document is filed. By contrast, no one knows what property passes to whom under a survivorship clause in a deed or other evidence of ownership.

In the case of decedents who died after December 31, 1981, where a husband and wife owned property in joint tenancy, with right of survivorship, the estate of the first spouse to die includes one-half of the value of the property, regardless of which spouse furnished the consideration for its acquisition. At first flush, this appears to be good news for married couples, as it eliminates the sometimes impossible job of endeavoring to trace the financial history of the property and prove the relative contribution of each spouse. On the other hand, the first spouse to die may have paid little if any of the cost, so that his/her gross estate may include half the value of property that had been obtained through the work or purchase of the survivor. Where property has increased in value since acquisition, the tax cost or basis for determining gain or loss on subsequent sale by the surviving spouse will be valued at the time of death or six months later, as elected by the executor, in the case of inherited property. Where the husband dies first, his assumed one-half of the property will have a stepped-up basis in the hands of his surviving spouse, while the half she is assumed to own will have its cost as its basis. If more than one-half of the property is presumed to be the husband's here, a greater part (perhaps all) of the property will receive a stepped-up basis. Where the 50-50 split provided by the Economic Recovery Tax Act of 1981 is not what the parties want, consideration should be given to changing these proportions by such means as interspousal gifts, which can now be regarded as tax-free under most circumstances.

4. Debt: In some states, certain jointly owned property is beyond the reach of the creditors of a deceased co-owner.

Joint ownership isn't always desirable

There are some disadvantages in joint ownership of property:

1. A major shortcoming of joint ownership is that on the death of one co-owner, the Internal Revenue Service as a matter of expediency considers that the decedent really owned all of the property and includes its value in his/her gross estate, then leaves the executor to prove the extent to which all of this property wasn't the decedent's—if he/she can. For failure of

adequate proof, the total value of property in which the decedent was only one co-owner frequently winds up in his/her gross estate even though the other co-owner(s) may actually have paid for their interests with their own funds. Proof of who furnished how much of the consideration many years ago is difficult, especially if the property was acquired piecemeal. This rule no longer applies to joint interests of husband and wife; now one-half of such property is included in the estate of the first spouse to die.

2. The death of a co-owner may make all of the property unavailable to the survivor for a time. For example, in the case of a joint bank account, the funds are frozen by the bank until the tax authorities unfreeze the account. Sale of property held in joint ownership with a decedent also entails many problems.

3. There can be serious practical problems in selling one's interest in property if co-owners are opposed to the idea.

4. If two or more persons jointly own property, such as a business, the Internal Revenue Service can shut down the entire enterprise for nonpayment of taxes by one co-owner.

5. If a husband and wife own property jointly, and there is a divorce, or even if there are marital difficulties that haven't gone that far, management and administration of the joint property can prove difficult.

6. Where certain types of property are owned jointly, one owner can be heavily involved financially because of an act of the co-owner. For example, if a mother and son own an automobile jointly and he gets involved in an accident that results in more money than the insurance covers, she is confronted with the liability because the accident was caused by her property.

7. When there's a joint bank account, one spouse cannot logically

argue that he/she didn't know what was in the account. This greatly weakens any claim, for example, that if the husband omits income from a joint return, the wife is not subject to tax, penalty, and interest on the unreported income because she is an innocent spouse.

Forms of joint ownership

These are the principal forms of joint ownership of property:

1. Joint tenancy. Each of the parties has an undivided interest in the entire property, so that if one owner dies, the survivor or survivors own the property. Each party reports the income from his/her portion of the property.

2. Tenancy in common. Each person owns a specified portion of the property. Upon the death of one party, his/her interest goes to his estate rather than to the surviving co-owner(s).

3. Tenancy by the entirety. This form of ownership applies only to legally married couples, and in some states it applies only to real estate. Each spouse has an undivided interest in the entire property, and on the death of one spouse, the survivor doesn't succeed to the decedent's right and title because she already had it. Half of the value of the property goes to the estate of the first to die. Upon sale of the property by the couple, gain or loss is divided between the spouses.

4. Community property. In eight states that have enacted community property laws, each spouse is deemed to own one-half of the property acquired by the other spouse after the marriage took place or after they moved into the state.

Federal gift tax

Federal gift tax may apply to the creation or termination of a joint-ownership arrangement. In general, if a person is given an interest in property without paying for it, or the consideration paid is less than the value of what is received, there is a taxable gift. If a father opens a joint bank account with his daughter, providing all the funds for it, or if he sets up a joint brokerage account to which he supplies all of the securities and cash, he has not made a taxable gift until such time as she withdraws or makes use of what he has put into the joint account.

Where two persons hold property as joint tenants (other than spouses' realty tenancies by the entirety or joint tenancies with right of survivorship), there is a taxable gift if one party contributed more of the purchase price than the other did. A gift also results if a joint tenancy is terminated and the proceeds of the sale of the property are divided among the parties in unequal amounts.

References to "taxable gift," of course, must be considered while recognizing the fact that because of the annual exclusion, available unified-estate- and gift-tax credit, and 100 percent gift-tax marital deductions, no tax may actually be due.

Federal income tax

Where co-owned property is sold, each co-owner generally has gain or loss measured by the difference between his/her basis (tax cost) in the property and his/her share of the realization.

Deaths in common disaster

When two joint tenants die under circumstances where it is not possible to determine the sequence of the deaths, the property so held is generally distributable one-half as if one co-owner had survived and one-half as if the other co-owner had survived. (See Chapter Seventeen, "Simultaneous Deaths of Spouses.")

Conclusions and advice

• Be prepared to show that the decedent had not furnished all of the consideration for the purchase of property by documenting what the co-owners had furnished of their own funds.

• Where husband and wife own property jointly, make provisions for the disposition of the property should both spouses die simultaneously. Their wills could contain certain alternative dispositions to meet this possibility.

• Do not use joint ownership as a substitute for a will. Very likely, all property won't be jointly owned, and in the absence of a will this is distributable according to the state's law of intestacy. In addition, a will is far more flexible and is subject to modification as family structure and other circumstances change. A survivor, moreover, may not be competent to handle all of the property that may be dumped on her/him by reason of the death of the co-owner. Perhaps a trust could be used effectively here.

• Do not use a joint ownership form if there is reason to believe that the co-owners, such as a husband and wife, are not likely to continue in a cordial relationship.

Chapter Nineteen

SALE-AND-LEASEBACK; GIFT-AND-LEASEBACK

An individual can reduce what would otherwise become his/her gross estate by immediately disposing of property that he now owns and uses in his trade or profession; but he can retain the business use of this property. At the same time, if the transaction is properly planned, he will be able to achieve income tax and other advantages. The mechanism for this is a sale-and-leaseback. Somewhat analogous to the sale-and-leaseback is another situation, the gift-and-leaseback.

Nature of a sale-and-leaseback transaction

Under a sale-and-leaseback, business property is sold, most advisedly to a completely independent party, here called "the investor" for the sake of simplicity. At the same time, the original owner leases back this property, usually for a long period of years. When he dies, the value of the property will not be includable in his gross estate, for he doesn't own the assets. But he has continued to have the use of somebody else's property in return for the payment of rent, which for federal income-tax purposes is deductible as a business expense.

A sale-and-leaseback with an unrelated party can be structured to meet the tax—and other—preferences of the parties.

The seller (the original owner of the business property) has these principal alternatives:

1. If his property has appreciated in value since acquisition, he can sell it at cost, thereby avoiding tax on the appreciation. Inasmuch as the investor has acquired the property at a bargain price, the simultaneous leaseback will call for this differential to be balanced out by means of a low rental to be paid over the life of the lease. In arrangements of this kind between unrelated parties, the one who pays too much or too little in terms of fair market value will have this differential adjusted in the form of the rental payments, adjusted high or low, so that what each party gives and gets over the life of the lease is substantially equivalent. The terms take into account the fact that an interest factor balances present payment of purchase price with rental payments over a period of years. For example, if the leaseback is for a period of 20 years, there are tables that disclose the present value of a dollar payable in 20 years.

2. Where the original owner sells his property at a loss and then leases it back, he is entitled to deduct a loss for tax purposes.

3. Property may be sold by the original owner for more than market value if he is in a low tax bracket for that year, or if he is operating at a loss. In such circumstances, the gain is not important to him taxwise. But

the simultaneous leaseback will provide for a high rental to compensate the buyer for the inflated price.

4. If the property includes land, the original owner would not have been able to deduct depreciation on the land. But after the leaseback, he deducts the rent paid on both the land and the building. He is, moreover, rid of the problems and nuisance of depreciation records and the arguments he would probably incur with the Internal Revenue Service.

Sale-and-leaseback transactions increase the seller's liquidity.

A sale-and-leaseback is not recognized for tax purposes by the Internal Revenue Service if the original owner retains any rights in the property other than the use of it in return for the payment of rent. The transaction must be a genuine sale. But in a 1979 decision, a court recognized as bona fide a sale-and-leaseback in which the original owner had been granted an option to repurchase the property by the investor.

The parties must be unrelated

For reasons discussed earlier, the original owner may be selling the property for more or less than its fair market value, and in consequence, paying rent that is higher or lower than would be the case in a customary sale or a conventional lease. But as long as the parties are not related, these arrangements are acceptable for tax purposes. Unrelated parties can bargain in an unconventional manner as long as each party achieves his/her own purposes without regard to what the other is seeking. But transactions of this nature with related parties should be avoided. Even if a party sells and then leases back property to a related party at the identical terms offered by an outside party, the Internal Revenue Service will predictably take the position that where assets are sold to a related party at an off-market price, or rented at an unrealistic figure in terms of standard practices, the consideration or expense can be readjusted for tax purposes. That is, if the rent paid to a related party is more than would have been charged on a standard lease, the excess can be disallowed.

Nature of a gift-and-leaseback transaction

Less common than the sale-and-leaseback is the gift-and-leaseback. This transaction may involve related parties if the terms are set at arm's length. Or it may involve a charitable organization.

A father may own property that he uses in his business or profession. As mentioned in an earlier chapter, a physician may own the building in which he practices, which also contains costly medical equipment. He gives the property to his children, thus reducing his ultimate gross estate. But he needs these facilities in his practice, so he immediately leases them back. His annual rental payments are deductible as business expenses. The income, received by the children, will presumably be taxed at a much lower rate than the doctor's when he takes the tax deduction.

But in order to gain the tax advantages from situations like this, it is vital that the original owner really let go of the property and that the rental payments be fair to the children, who may not be in a position to bargain for an equitable rental. For this reason, it would be advisable for the physician to transfer the property in trust for the benefit of his children. The trustee or trustees should be completely independent of the domination of the original owner, so that they can bargain with him as to a fair rental and refuse any figure that doesn't seem to be in the children's interest. All too frequently, transactions of this kind are not recognized for tax purposes because the original owner set the rent, or served as trustee, or selected trustees who really represented him and not the children. For example, the transaction wasn't recognized for tax purposes where the trustees were the three persons whom the original owner regarded most highly: his lawyer, his accountant, and himself. The two professionals merely acquiesced in whatever their longtime client wanted. The property was thus includable in his gross estate.

Where a gift-and-leaseback involves the owner's children, the rental payments he makes cannot be used to discharge his legal obligation of supporting minor children.

An individual similarly reduces his ultimate gross estate if he donates property used in his trade or business to an approved charitable organization and simultaneously leases back the facilities. He gets a charitable deduction for the value of the property used for the contribution. His annual rental expenses are also deductible.

Motivation for transaction

The motivation for the transaction—even if it takes advantage of a tax opportunity—is immaterial if the donor retains no control over the property.

Conclusions and advice

- To find an independent investor for a sale-and-leaseback, read brokers' advertisements in the financial sections of newspapers.
- Let go of the property and reacquire an interest solely as tenant.

• Where property is given or sold to one's minor children, use a trust with a truly independent trustee.

• Do not enter into a sale-and-leaseback with a related party even at terms identical to those offered by an outside party.

• Do not attempt to make any unilateral modification of the arrangement.

Chapter Twenty

RECAPITALIZING A CORPORATION

If a substantial portion of an individual's assets consists of stock in a closely-held corporation, the tax consequences of his eventual death should be minimized by one or more of several available plans. If this person plans to minimize the amount of what will become his gross estate, he should consider making gifts of assets to his beneficiaries. Additionally, or alternatively, he may make gifts to approved charitable organizations currently for deductions on his federal income-tax return. Or he can make charitable bequests that will constitute deductions in arriving at his taxable estate. (See Chapter Thirty-four, "Charitable Deductions That Benefit the Family.")

Where retention of control seems to rule out stock gifts

The making of such gifts, contributions, or charitable bequests is a standard method of reducing what will be one's gross estate at the time of death. But in the case of a significant stock interest in a closely-held corporation, the idea is usually unattractive. Possession of all, most, or even a large portion of the voting stock of a corporation enables a person to control—or at least participate in the control of—his business. He doesn't want to give up this control or even dilute it to any meaningful degree. His control of the company's voting stock enables him to make business decisions, name the directors and the executives of the company, choose his successors, and have a major role in setting his own salary, bonus, and fringe benefits. He wants to retain the stock, even if it means paying unnecessarily high estate and perhaps income taxes.

Here is a practical alternative that is useful when, as is usually the case, a closely-held corporation has only one class of stock outstanding. The plan is equally attractive if the corporation is capitalized with common stock that carries the voting power, plus preferred stock.

Recapitalization offers opportunities

The directors can vote to have a recapitalization from the existing one-class stock into two new classes of stock, voting and nonvoting. If there are both common and preferred shares outstanding, the recapitalization will involve a reshuffling from the old common into new common of two types, which may be identical except that only one of these classes has voting power. An attorney can easily take care of the formalities of this recapitalization, which can be a "Type E" tax-free reorganization. That is, the shareholders will not have to pay federal income tax when they surrender their old shares and receive new ones.

When a major stockholder's shares are exchanged for the new ones—for example, old one-class voting stock for new voting common shares and new nonvoting common shares—the tax value of his investment in the shares of the corporation remains exactly as it was before the recapitalization. But the basis of his investment now is apportioned between the new voting stock and the new nonvoting stock. The services of an experienced accountant are usually necessary to apportion the tax cost of the investment between the new voting and the new nonvoting shares.

The stockholder will keep his new voting shares, for they represent a control over the corporation that, understandably, he doesn't want to relinquish. He gives the nonvoting shares to his beneficiaries, perhaps in gifts over a period of years in order to minimize the tax on these gifts through the annual gift-tax exclusion and husband-wife split gifts. (See Chapter Eight, "Gifts Still Have Advantages.")

This tax-free recapitalization into voting and nonvoting shares assures that an important stockholder retains what is probably the most important thing to him: his voting control of—or at least a voting interest in—the corporation. What he will then have in his gross estate when he dies is only that portion of the stock's total value that has been apportioned by the accountant to the voting stock, assuming that the accountant has utilized a procedure that is generally accepted. Usually this is the total value of the individual's investment in the company, apportioned between voting and nonvoting shares on the basis of their respective values. For example, the actual figures might indicate that voting stock represented 40 percent and nonvoting stock 60 percent of the new capitalization. The value of the nonvoting stock the individual gives away before the time of his eventual death won't be part of his gross estate when he dies. He has managed to reduce his estate without any loss of control of the corporation.

Why stop at one recapitalization?

This method need not be regarded as a one-time benefit. In a later year, if inflation or the corporation's financial success has brought the value of the stockholder's new voting stock to a figure that would swell the value of his gross estate unduly, there can be a second recapitalization. This will once more bring down the value of his voting stock because of the apportionment of total value between his existing stock and the new nonvoting stock.

Other uses of recapitalizations

A recapitalization may also be utilized to bring down the value, and therefore the price, of voting stock so that some of it can be sold to employees at a price they can afford. This would provide them with incentive to remain with the company and to work more energetically for its success—they now own a piece of the action.

A decedent's gross estate includes the value of stock he had transferred to an irrevocable trust in which he retained no benefit to himself, if he continued to own, directly or indirectly, shares possessing at least 20 percent of the corporation's voting rights. A capitalization could be used so that he received some nonvoting stock, thereby enabling him to transfer voting stock to a trust for the benefit of his children. They could receive the voting shares when they reach a specified age.

As shareholders who are actively in control of a company get older, a recapitalization from the existing one-class voting stock will enable the more mature shareholders to receive preferred stock with its relatively safe fixed dividend. The voting common would go to younger persons who are assuming greater responsibilities in the corporation and who should therefore be entitled to the higher dividends that their management might bring about.

As a person gets older or his health deteriorates, a capitalization may be used to protect the voting-stock interest he chooses to retain in the corporation to assure his salary determination and the like. New voting stock can be made available to proven executives who will take over increasing responsibilities so that the corporation won't suffer from the aging shareholder's diminishing capabilities. Meanwhile, his investment is protected.

Recapitalization and the marital deduction

An individual may provide by will that his one-class stock go to his wife and children in specified amounts. The will may further provide that when he dies a recapitalization will be effected under stipulated terms, so that his widow's shares will be replaced with preferred stock of equal par value. In one such situation, the preferred stock received by the surviving spouse qualified for the marital deduction. (See Chapter Fourteen, "The Marital Deduction.") This was true even though the preferred stock did not exist at the moment of the husband's death, the recapitalization remaining uneffected until after he died. Her preferred stock interest had been created by the will and, therefore, passed from the decedent to her.

Recapitalization may be at the bidding of a third party

Sometimes it is necessary to recapitalize in order to preserve the value of an inherited bequest. For example, a decedent might have left to his wife or children a valuable automobile distributorship franchise he owned and operated. Frequently such a franchise agreement provides that upon the death of the principal operator, the franchise will be canceled by the manufacturer unless the principal is succeeded by an experienced person acceptable to the manufacturer. Predictably, the distributor's widow and children would not be acceptable. So there is a recapitalization, the family getting preferred or nonvoting common as well as a minority interest in the common stock. Most of the voting stock is made available to persons who are acceptable to the manufacturer and appear likely to keep the franchise operating successfully. Without this recapitalization, a valuable franchise may be lost.

Sometimes a bank refuses to continue or extend a credit agreement to a corporation on the death of its guiding spirit unless a similar arrangement is made.

Conclusions and advice

• Use experienced tax counsel in structuring the corporate recapitalization. A knowledgeable accountant should allocate the tax basis between the new stock issues.

• Tax-free recapitalizations may be utilized several times throughout the years to obtain the benefits described in this chapter.

• Do not assume that because an individual's wealth is primarily tied up in his corporation, his opportunities for estate planning and making charitable contributions are limited.

• Do not confine the advantages of a tax-free recapitalization to estate-planning benefits. Such a recapitalization may also be utilized for present tax benefits, to induce key employees to remain with the company, as well as to assure the renewal of corporate franchises and bank-credit agreements.

• Do not assume that all recapitalizations are tax-free; they aren't. Professional guidance is advisable to assure tax-free status.

• Restructuring can bring in parties with whom you do not wish to associate for either business or personal purposes. You must consider whether "new names" will jeopardize your carefully built-up reputation for integrity and trustworthiness.

Chapter Twenty-one

REDEMPTION OF STOCK TO PAY DEATH TAXES

The death of someone who owns all or a large proportion of the shares of a closely-held corporation presents a serious problem: What is to be done with his/her stock?

Money will be required to pay bills, the federal estate tax, and the requirements of the beneficiaries under the will. The family or other beneficiaries may prefer to get what is designated for them in cash rather than in the form of an investment in a business that they don't understand and lack the experience to direct. The remaining shareholders of the corporation, if there be such, might be disinclined to accept as co-owners the spouse, children, or other relatives of the decedent. Banks and other parties with which the corporation has been dealing may be unwilling to continue to deal with an enterprise that now has unproven persons in positions of authority. Employees are apt to be demoralized at the thought of having outsiders outrank them.

The need to sell a decedent's stock

In many instances, the obvious situation would be for the executor or the beneficiaries to sell their stock. But to whom, and at what price? Shares of a closely-held corporation are a highly unmarketable commodity—who knows the true state of the organization or the value of the stock? This is especially important where, as often happens, there has never been a complete thorough examination of the books by an independent certified public accountant. If the decedent's stock represented less than a controlling interest in the corporation, the problem of marketability becomes even more serious. Who would buy stock in a closely-held corporation where he wouldn't be able to apply his own expertise and genius to the problems because the other shareholders might resent an outsider?

So if the executor or beneficiaries could find a potential buyer at all, the price would have to be distressingly low.

Corporation's purchase of a decedent's shares may be dividend, unless...

The logical market for the decedent's shares would be the corporation itself. But federal income-tax law provides that any money flowing from a corporation to a shareholder at a time when the company has sufficient earnings and profits to pay a dividend will be taxed as a dividend—that is, as ordinary income and not as capital gain. There are a few specific exceptions to this rule: For example, when all of a stockholder's stock is acquired and he completely terminates his relationship with the corporation. Such would be the case when a shareholder dies, of course, but the rule also provides that all shares of certain closely related persons must be taken into account in determining whether the redemption satisfies some highly technical rules. So this solution is not available in most situations where the decedent's immediate family members also own some stock, even a single share.

A ready purchaser for a decedent's stock

There is a method by which a decedent's stock may be purchased by the issuing corporation without dividend implications to the seller. But if this method is to be put into operation after the shareholder's death, advance planning is necessary.

Federal tax law provides that the proceeds of a sale of stock to the corporation will not be taxed as a dividend to the extent that the money is used to pay death taxes and the estate's administrative expenses. Any amount paid by the corporation to the seller in excess of this amount will be taxed as a dividend. Under the Tax Reform Act of 1986, none of the amount of the redemption will be treated as capital gain; everything is now ordinary income. But this is treated as a sale of stock, which means that the proceeds will be reduced for tax purposes by the basis (usually cost) of the stock instead of being fully taxable as a dividend.

The tax law refers to this sale of stock back to the issuing corporation as a "distribution in redemption of stock to pay death taxes." But the stock doesn't actually have to be redeemed in the ordinary sense—that is, canceled by the corporation. For this purpose, it is immaterial what happens to the shares after the company buys them back. They may be held by the corporation as treasury stock. They may be transferred to other persons or resold. The proceeds of the redemption, however, must be used for (a) the paying of any tax resulting from the death of the decedent, including federal estate tax and any state inheritance, legacy, or succession tax, and (b) administrative expenses of the estate.

A crucial test

However, even if the proceeds of redemption are used only for such costs, there is another paramount consideration. In order for the purchase of its own stock by the corporation not to result in a dividend to the estate or beneficiaries, the value of the stock included in the decedent's gross estate must exceed 35 percent of the total value of the gross estate beyond expenses, obligations, taxes, and losses of the estate.

In applying this percentage test, the value of all the decedent's stock in the corporation is considered—not merely the value of the shares of the particular class of stock to be redeemed, such as voting common. Accordingly, if the total value of both the common and preferred stock of a corporation owned by an estate meets the percentage test, but neither common nor preferred alone meets it, the redemption of either class up to the permissible limitation qualifies for nondividend treatment.

Sometimes a decedent's shares in any one corporation won't qualify for this 35 percent rule because his/her investments took the form of substantial holdings in several companies. Where the estate includes stock of two or more corporations, in each of which the decedent had a 20 percent or greater interest, these companies may be regarded as a single corporation for this purpose.

The redemption by the corporation must be made within three years and 90 days after the filing date of the federal estate-tax return. If the executor and the Internal Revenue Service are not in agreement about the amount of tax payable, the permissible period for redemption of stock is extended until 60 days after the decision of the tax court becomes final. Whichever party loses there can appeal to a higher court, so the appeals procedure can keep the redemption period open for a considerable period of time. For this reason, an executor may not know how much stock to present to the corporation for redemption without dividend implications. When the estate-tax return is filed, enough stock to pay the indicated tax and administrative expenses may be redeemed. If the IRS or a court subsequently decides that more tax is due, additional shares can be redeemed without dividend implications within the above time limits.

In order to reap the benefits of this chapter, the executor should understand that stock must be redeemed within the permissible period; it does no good to learn about it too late. In one case, a judge declared: "It would appear to me...that in a given circumstance it would not be untoward for an agent of the IRS to point out to a taxpayer that there is a benefit (in redeeming stock to pay death taxes) that could be taken advantage of...." But don't count on getting such a suggestion.

In determining whether a decedent owned sufficient shares in a particular corporation to qualify for nondividend treatment, only the value of shares owned directly by him is taken into account. Accordingly, in ascertaining whether a decedent owned more than 35 percent of the stock of Corporation A, there cannot be included any shares of A which were owned by Corporation B, even if he owned 90 percent of the stock of

Corporation B. But any shares owned by a trust the decedent created will be included, if he is deemed to have retained at the time of his death such a degree of control over the trust that he hadn't let go of the property that he had transferred to it.

Funding

A certain amount of planning is necessary to take advantage of this provision of the tax law. Sufficient funds must be available so that the corporation will be able to buy the stock if and when it is presented for redemption. This funding is frequently arranged by taking out insurance on shareholders' lives just for this purpose. (See Chapter Twenty-two, "Buy-Sell Agreements.") Or a corporation might be able to borrow money to redeem a shareholder's stock at the time of his death if it has not retained income for that purpose.

If the corporation retains earnings that have been earmarked to redeem a decedent's shares under circumstances that qualify as a redemption of stock to pay death taxes, the retained earnings are not subject to the accumulated earnings tax of up to 38 percent of undistributed profits for that tax year.

Advance planning

An accountant should probably check the figures periodically to ascertain whether a shareholder's stock interest in a particular corporation exceeds 35 percent of his adjusted gross estate—that is, the portion of his estate necessary for taking advantage of the nondividend treatment discussed in this section. That means (a) estimating the approximate value of adjusted gross estate and (b) determining the value of the stock. If (b) does not exceed 35 percent of (a), take steps to see that it does. This can be done in either of two ways. First, reduce the size of what the estate will be by making gifts or charitable contributions in the form of other property, including money. Second, acquire additional shares of stock in the corporation so that, while the size of the estate remains the same, the stock interest it holds will be greater.

Although there is no longer a requirement that gifts within three years of death be included in the estate, such gifts will be taken into account in deciding whether the 35 percent requirement has been met.

Conclusions and advice

• Do not have a corporation redeem a deceased shareholder's stock unless this qualifies as a redemption to pay death taxes. Otherwise the proceeds may be taxed as a dividend.

• Have your accountant check regularly to be certain that your shares in a closely-held corporation will qualify for redemption on a nondividend basis. If not, compliance may be affected by reducing your gross estate, or by acquiring more stock.

• Take steps to ensure that the corporation will be in a position to fund a redemption of stock to pay death taxes. It could be your estate that will benefit from this.

• Do not cause a corporation to retain earnings to buy a decedent's shares unless the transaction has been set up so as to qualify as a redemption to pay death taxes. Otherwise the corporation will probably be subjected to the accumulated earnings tax.

Chapter Twenty-two

BUY-SELL AGREEMENTS

The death of a shareholder in a closely-held corporation brings massive problems to the estate and its executor—but not only to them. There are immediate matters of concern to a variety of other parties, one of which is the omnipresent Internal Revenue Service. Whether or not the corporation continues to exist may depend on the effective solution of these problems.

• Burden of proof. The estate has the responsibility of valuing the shares for tax purposes. This is a chore that may seem to have no solution that is acceptable to the IRS, for here fair market value can't be determined by actual sales of stock, which in all probability had never taken place in a truly arm's-length transaction. The taxpayer has the burden of proof of establishing a valuation; without evidence of actual sales, the IRS can come up with an extraordinarily high figure by comparing the stock with that of far more prestigious companies with diversified product lines, depth in top management, and the like.

Unless the executor can prove the validity of the stock value he/she uses, the IRS's finding will prevail. The IRS can make computations based upon various commonly accepted valuation methods, such as capitalized earnings per share, choosing whichever of these generally accepted methods produces the highest figure in a particular instance. In addition, the executor also has to assemble the cash necessary to pay the federal estate tax, usually nine months after the date of the decedent's death.

• Executor's personal tax liability. The beneficiaries may require immediate funds, without being able to wait until their inheritances can be processed. But hasty distribution of bequests by an executor can involve him/her in personal tax liability that he may seek to minimize by being unduly deliberate and hesitant. Additionally, some beneficiaries will now, or very soon, have shares of stock that may be difficult to convert to cash.

• Employee uneasiness. The corporation's employees might reasonably fear that the company will be liquidated because the estate has no other way of raising cash or because of dissension among old and new shareholders. This fear of loss of jobs could result in employee uneasiness and affect the corporation's performance adversely.

• Lenders at bay. Creditors are likely to be worried that beneficiaries without experience or judgment will take over the running of the business, with disastrous results. One lender required a company seeking a loan to insure the life of the chief executive and primary stockholder "so that if anything happened to him the company would have capital to reorganize or to put somebody else in his place."

The solution: a buyout agreement

Managers of closely-held corporations should take steps to protect themselves against the loss of key shareholders. An excellent way of doing so is to plan a buyout agreement.

This arrangement can take either of two forms. In a buy-and-sell agreement the stockholders, or certain designated ones, agree to purchase the shares of any party to the agreement who dies. In a stock-redemption agreement, the corporation itself buys the stock of the deceased shareholder.

Several alternative methods are available for setting the price to be paid for a decedent's stock. There may be an agreed dollar price per share, a method that is undesirable because, at the time the stock is actually purchased, that price may no longer be realistic. The agreed price might be book value per share. The figure might be obtained by capitalizing corporate earnings, the agreement to state the number of years' earnings to be used in the computation and the rate of capitalization. The amount could be set by a postmortem appraisal, although the resultant figure might be so different from what had been forecast that funding arrangements would be unworkable. Best of all would be a self-adjusting formula, such as average earnings of the past three years capitalized at 10 percent, or book value plus a goodwill factor to be determined by arbitration. The first of these methods appears more attractive in times of inflation.

Upon the death of a shareholder covered by the agreement, his/her shares would go to the other stockholders who were parties to the arrangement or, under a stock-redemption plan, to the corporation, which would retire the shares. The price would set the value of the shares for estate-tax purposes because it represented an actual sale determined by arm's-length negotiations among shareholders who, when the agreement was made, didn't know whether they (or their estates) would be sellers or buyers.

Funding

The agreement is meaningless without a guaranteed source of money with which to buy the decedent's stock. So if the corporation is to be the purchaser, it may insure the lives of each shareholder and use the proceeds to buy a decedent's stock at the formula price. If the other shareholders are to be the buyers, each one takes out insurance on his/her own life for this specific purpose. The policies can be assigned to a representative or trustee, and the proceeds will be used to purchase shares from the shareholder's estate.

If one of the shareholders is uninsurable, he/she could use insurance policies that were previously taken out. Alternatively, this person might be able to purchase substandard or high-risk insurance despite age or health risks, paying an appropriately high premium to compensate the insurance company for its extra hazard. Many insurance companies now write this type of coverage.

In this connection, a strong argument for having the corporation buy the stock is the fact that the corporation isn't likely to forget to pay the insurance premiums on the policy needed to pay for the redemption. If each shareholder carried insurance on his/her own life, he might "forget" to pay the premiums, save the money, and leave insufficient funding for the plan at death. Another argument in favor of having the corporation acquire the shares is that they can be retired. That is a great benefit to the remaining shareholders; each will still own the same number of shares of stock, but his/her percentage of ownership will be higher because the total number of shares has been reduced. Even though each shareholder now has a greater equity in the corporation, he/she isn't deemed to have received a dividend for tax purposes when the corporation pays the life insurance premiums or when a decedent's shares are retired.

The cost of premiums is not deductible for income-tax purposes. But a corporation can deduct the expense of legal fees to prepare a stock-repurchase agreement.

Consequences of a buyout agreement

Suppose that the premiums are neglected and on a shareholder's death there are insufficient funds with which to purchase all his/her shares. The plan need not have been a complete failure. At least some of the decedent's shares will have been purchased, and that generally sets a valuation of his/her stock for estate-tax purposes. It provides a certain amount of needed cash. And the agreement can be worded to provide that if there is insufficient cash generated by the plan to buy all of a decedent's stock, the corporation or the surviving shareholders will have an option to buy the remaining shares at later dates when cash becomes available, at a formula price.

The surviving spouse or other beneficiary receiving a decedent's shares may seek to refuse to honor the buyout agreement on the ground that she/he was never a party to it. That argument won't work, for she/he acquired the shares subject to the agreement and the formula price.

Nonvoting stock may be covered

Although only the voting stock is customarily covered, sometimes a buyout agreement can provide for the purchase of nonvoting common or preferred stock. This way, the decedent's family members are completely bought out. Acquisition of preferred or other nonvoting stock that is convertible into common shares should be provided for.

Total disability of stockholder

Although this is not a common practice, a buyout agreement may be utilized to cover the possibility of a shareholder's permanent disability in a closely-held corporation. He/she can probably use the cash, and the corporation's management may not want to have any of its stock in the hands of someone who is no longer actively involved in running the business. The shares might be better used to attract a new executive to take the place of the incapacitated individual.

Conclusions and advice

• Be prepared to show who the buyer in a buyout agreement actually is. If shareholders are obligated to purchase a decedent's stock but it turns out that the corporation actually buys it, the corporate payment will be taxed as a dividend to the shareholders. If the corporation is to be the buyer, you must be able to prove that it was a party to the agreement and that it actually received the shares.

• Have your accountant work out the application of the valuation formula each year. If changing values indicate that there won't be enough cash to purchase a decedent's stock, take out more life insurance to fund the plan. Or reduce the value of the voting stock to be purchased. (See Chapter Twenty, "Recapitalizing a Corporation.")

• Where there is a buy-sell agreement, have the restrictions on sale other than to the corporation or the surviving shareholders stamped on each stock certificate. This will allow you to avoid serious problems when a buyer of the stock argues that he/she was never given notice of the restrictions.

• Be careful that the operation of a buy-sell agreement doesn't reduce the number of shareholders to so few individuals that personal holding-company liability will exist. This could happen in the case of undistributed earnings should income be largely of a nonoperating type.

• Do not use a formula clause so complicated or vague that the decedent's family must ask a court to "interpret" what it means. This could lead to delays, unpleasant litigation, and a forced settlement.

• Don't overlook the fact that a properly funded buy-sell agreement can determine whether a corporation will be able to survive after the death of a shareholder.

• A buy-sell agreement is sometimes funded by life insurance (see page 134). If this is the case, consider and constantly review how good the insurance company is. There are rating agencies that will assist you in your evaluation. Consider possible alternatives if an insurance company can no longer honor its obligations.

• One taxpayer's argument that the terms of a buy-sell agreement should be binding were weakened because, when another stockholder previously had died, no one had paid any attention to the agreement.

Chapter Twenty-three

MERGER TO ESTABLISH ESTATE-TAX VALUATION

Valuation of the shares of a closely-held corporation can be a significant potential problem for anyone who owns a substantial block of them. Obviously, when a stock is not listed on a registered exchange or actively traded in a lively over-the-counter market, fair market value can't be easily established. Fair market value is defined as the price at which property changes hands in a transaction between a willing buyer and a willing seller, where each has knowledge of the relevant facts and neither is under any compulsion to buy or sell. Such a situation rarely exists in the case of shares of a closely-held corporation.

Exchange of stock can establish fair market value

Some owners of shares in a closely-held corporation are sufficiently worried about estate-tax-valuation problems after their deaths to liquidate the company. When they die, their estates will contain cash or marketable securities, the valuation and disposition of which lend themselves easily to determinable valuation and intelligent planning. But most corporations, unlike individuals, are worth more alive than dead; liquidation would lessen the value of one's investment. For example, going-concern value, goodwill, and carryovers would be lost. Nontransferable franchises or licenses would be forfeited. Not least, there could be federal income tax resulting from the liquidation.

The problem, then, is to replace the shares of closely-held corporation stock with shares that are readily susceptible to valuation. Then the Internal Revenue Service won't have the opportunity to fill a valuation vacuum with its own figures.

Under these circumstances, a desirable plan for the shareholder to adopt is an exchange of his/her shares in the closely-held corporation for stock in a company traded actively in a recognized market so that valuation at death will not be left to the IRS by default.

Tax-free reorganization can result in determinable value

Shares in the closely-held corporation can be exchanged for shares of an actively traded company through the mechanism of a tax-free reorganization. Then when the stockholder dies, his/her property will have a readily ascertainable value. This procedure will also enable a stockholder to formulate an intelligent estate plan, as hard figures to work with will at all times be available. All values are subject to fluctuations, of course. But an individual can plan his/her property dispositions, trust arrangements, marital deduction, gift-tax exclusions—among other matters discussed in this book—much more competently and intelligently if he/she has at least some idea of the value of the stocks and other properties that will be in his/her ultimate gross estate.

A individual can replace his/her shares in a closely-held corporation for stock in a better-known company without recognition of any taxable gain or loss, if the transaction complies with the requirements for a tax-free reorganization as contained in the Internal Revenue Code.

The forms of tax-free reorganization

The "A" type of reorganization involves a merger or consolidation. Particularly suitable here is a transaction in which a publicly-owned corporation acquires all of the stock of the closely-held company, which is then liquidated, the shareholders of the latter receiving shares of the continuing corporation.

The "B" reorganization involves the acquisition by the well-known company of at least 80 percent of the stock of the closely-held corporation, solely in exchange for some of the voting stock of the larger corporation. For the purpose of the present plan, it would be advisable for all of the stock of the closely-held corporation to be exchanged during the course of the transaction.

If the closely-held corporation has some valuable assets, a good cash flow, and an impressive earnings record, it is an attractive company for takeover purposes. But even if the closely-held company has had dismal earnings, with operating losses over several years, it may still be a useful acquisition. In certain types of reorganization, such as Type "A," if the ground rules are met, net operating losses of an acquired company can be utilized by the corporation that acquires its stock. (Admittedly, there are some formidable traps and restraints here, but these are the problems of the acquiring company and not of the money-losing company or its shareholders.)

Conclusions and advice

• The working out of a tax-free reorganization is highly technical and strewn with pitfalls. You would be well advised to employ the services of an attorney or accountant who is well versed in this complex area of specialization.*

• If your business is not incorporated, carry out this plan in two phases. First, transfer all of the assets and liabilities of your business to a corporation formed for the purpose in exchange for all of its stock. Your transfer of assets, even if they have greatly appreciated in value since you acquired them, will be tax-free in most situations; the person who advises you on the reorganization can point out the few areas where this isn't the case. Second, you then exchange the shares of this corporation for those of a better-known company.

• In order to find corporations whose stock has a readily ascertainable market value, consult a broker who specializes in acquisitions. These brokers frequently advertise in the Sunday financial section of *The New York Times* or in *The Wall Street Journal*.

• When exchanging the shares of your closely held corporation for the securities of a better-known company in a tax-free reorganization, do

---

*See also Robert S. Holzman, *Tax-Free Reorganization After the Pension Reform Act of 1974*, Farnsworth Publishing Company, 1976.

not accept any of the latter's bonds as part of the swap unless you are surrendering bonds of your own company. Receipt of a larger principal amount of bonds than you give up (which could well be zero) is regarded as taxable income in most instances.

• Do not accept cash as part of the exchange, for this can have tax consequences.

• Be aware that in a merger, you may lose control of your business. Or you may end up with disagreeable or overly aggressive fellow stockholders who are difficult to work with.

Chapter Twenty-four

BUSINESS-CONTINUATION ARRANGEMENTS

There are several reasons an individual might want to have his business continued after his death:

• He believes that he has created or developed an enterprise that will provide a good source of income for his beneficiaries. In times of inflation, they might benefit more from a proven, ongoing business than from investments purchased with the proceeds of its disposition.

• He would like his children to step into executive positions at the appropriate time, without being subject to a lengthy and unpredictable climb up the executive ladder. Thus their principal inheritances from him may be, at some point in time yet unknown, the business he feels that he is developing for them.

• He realizes that most businesses are worth more alive, as going ventures, than could be realized from their liquidation. If the business died with him, his beneficiaries wouldn't receive the full value of what he owned at the time of his death.

Executors are likely to frustrate decedent's wishes

After the owner of a business dies, his executors may try to dispose of the venture as quickly as possible. The executors may not be familiar with the business; if they are, they may not want to deal with the many problems that go with it. They may be anxious to wind up the estate, distribute its assets, obtain their fees, and resume their normal activities.

As a result, the business will be sold or dissolved with all deliberate speed. *How much* may not be as important to the executors in agreeing to a price as *how quickly*.

Decedent's wishes should control

Yet estate planning should not be based upon making life easier for the decedent's executors. If disposition or liquidation of the business is not what the owner wants, he/she must take appropriate steps to prevent it.

The plan: Remove the business from what will be property subject to the administration of—and disposition by—the executors. Whether the business is a proprietorship or a controlling-stock interest in a corporation, the method is the same. Arrange to transfer the business interest to a trust created solely for this purpose: a business-continuation trust. The owner can do this at any time by a deed of trust (an inter vivos trust). But since he probably wants to manage the business for as long as he lives, he may prefer to postpone matters and have the business interest transferred to a trust in accordance with provisions in his will (a testamentary trust).

Who should operate your business when you die

Executors are usually chosen because they are people the testator trusts and admires for certain personal characteristics: interest in and concern for his family or other beneficiaries, devotion to the objectives and aspirations of the decedent, psychological understanding of the personalities involved, patience. The fiduciaries of the trust set up to continue the administration of the business, however, should be chosen for two characteristics:

1. They have the professional capacity to run the business with a high degree of efficiency.

2. They are committed to running it.

Character of the trust

The trustees could be chosen from among individuals who are already highly knowledgeable about the business. Possible candidates are its accounting adviser, attorney, the bank officer who handles financing and credit matters, perhaps a senior executive or a key employee of the company. Others who might be selected are management consultants or retired executives of other companies in this particular field.

The trust would be set up for the benefit of designated parties, which could include not only individuals but approved charitable organizations. The trust may be established with a life span of specified duration, such as until the grantor's youngest child reaches a stated age, most frequently 21, and is competent to take over the business as remainderman, or one of the remaindermen, when the trust has reached its termination date. But a certain amount of discretion may well be lodged in the trustees as to termination of the trust. The business might experience financial adversity, perhaps because of the loss of its guiding spirit, perhaps because of changing economic or legal factors. It might be unwise to require the trustees to continue the enterprise when, in their collective judgment, the venture was hopeless by reason of new foreign competition, environmental restrictions, expiration of an essential franchise, and the like. So the trustees could be vested with authority to sell or liquidate the business under specified circumstances, such as the incurring of operating losses in two or three successive years.

Permanent disability

Estate planning usually refers to what will take place when an individual dies. But the same plan may be essential in the case of his permanent disability; after a heart attack, stroke, or serious injury, he may be as unequal to the financial and economic demands he had formerly coped with as though he were indeed dead. An individual's business may suffer as grievously from his permanent disability as from his death. A business-continuation trust could be set up, to become operational at such time as a person is permanently disabled, either physically or mentally. A prudent planner might anticipate this possibility, however remote it seems, and have the necessary trust agreement drawn up, with only names and dates to be filled in when and if necessary.

Conclusions and advice

• Do not assume that your executors will continue to administer your business after you die. Most executors wish to relieve themselves of this responsibility as soon as possible. Are your devoted and trustworthy executors actually competent to run a complex business in today's environment? Do they have the expertise to engage the proper persons to take over the administration and planning of your business?

• Make certain that the business-continuation trust is carefully thought out in advance. Some vital considerations: who the trustees will be, provision for substitute or successor trustees, how long you want the trustees to administer the business, a safety-valve provision if the enterprise loses money regularly or is no longer competitive. Sound out the trustees you have in mind to ascertain whether they will serve and are agreeable to working with the other designated trustees.

• Do not require the trustees to continue the business if in their collective judgment there is no future in it. Example: Trustees may be directed to continue the business until the grantor's youngest child is 21. By the time that occurs, the industry may be in a hopeless condition. Leave discretion to terminate the business to a majority of the trustees, who should state in writing why this seems to be necessary.

Chapter Twenty-five

PLANNING WITH LIFE INSURANCE

There is no easier way to provide an estate after your death than to take out insurance on your life. Then if you keep paying the premiums and arrange matters—as you can through a trust—so that no creditor is able to attach the value of the policy, you are certain to leave an estate. Even these two qualifications can be dealt with. Arrangements can be made with an insurance company—sometimes they are automatic—that if premiums are missed, they will be paid from accumulated cash values or by conversion to another form of insurance.

What is deemed to be life insurance

Most forms of life insurance require the applicant to have a physical examination, so the implementation of your plan to create an estate through insurance should not be unduly delayed. The longer the delay, the greater is the possibility that you will become uninsurable. Generally group insurance doesn't call for a physical examination, nor does flight insurance, although the Supreme Court has called the latter a form of life insurance despite the absence of an examination. If the insurance company's doctor labels you uninsurable, all is not necessarily lost. Speak to your insurance adviser about the possibility of obtaining high-risk insurance. Regardless of your physical condition, you'll probably be able to get the insurance, but at a premium reflecting the degree of risk the insurance company faces.

Start coverage as early as possible

Unlike other forms of estate building, such as through realty or investments, the creation of an estate through life insurance doesn't require the attainment of a degree of business or financial success that might take many years to achieve. The size of an insurance estate depends upon how much an individual is willing or able to pay in premiums. (In many situations, insurance premiums are paid by an employer, in whole or in part.) How much insurance you carry may depend on the form of policy you purchase. For the same amount of premium, for example, you can acquire far greater coverage with term insurance than with straight life or endowment forms.

You should ask yourself what you are really purchasing, life insurance (which includes the building up of cash values, reinvestment and borrowing power, enforced savings, interesting conversion privileges) or death insurance (which provides indemnity in case of the death of the insured and nothing else). One person wants to buy insurance protection for his entire life. Another individual is seeking coverage for a specified period of time only, perhaps until his/her children reach the age of financial independence or his/her newly established business has had time to develop.

The federal income tax

In most instances, insurance proceeds payable by reason of the death of the insured are excluded from gross income, whether received by the estate, a beneficiary, a transferee, or anyone else. But the interest element in an insurance company's settlement option may be taxable. For example, after the death of the insured, the beneficiary may have selected a settlement option calling for the payment of a certain dollar amount for life. What he/she receives represents in part an amortized portion of the principal sum to which he/she is entitled plus interest on the principal that still remains in the hands of the insurance company.

The federal estate tax

Unlike other forms of property, none of the value of an insurance estate needs to be includable in a decedent's gross estate at the time of death. In fact, if an individual knows the simple ground rules, insurance proceeds will not be a part of his gross estate unless he wants them to be to provide his executor(s) with liquidity. Proceeds of insurance on the life of a decedent are includable in his gross estate only if (a) he had named the estate or the executor as the beneficiary, (b) he had given away the policy within three years of the time of his death, or (c) at the moment of his death he had held an incident of ownership of the policy, exercisable either alone or in conjunction with someone else.

The most common forms of incidents of ownership are the right to change the name of the beneficiary, to assign the policy or cancel it, or to pledge the policy in order to obtain a loan.

Relinquishment of any of these rights within three years of death will not take the proceeds out of the estate. That the decedent had been unable to relinquish these rights is irrelevant. For example, a policy's terms can be changed only by endorsement of the policy itself by the insurance company, but the policy is physically in the hands of a hostile person, such as an estranged wife. Or a traveler might purchase flight insurance that automatically names the purchaser as owner; should the plane crash, even if he/she has had time to change the name of the owner, the proceeds are still part of his/her gross estate—the three-year rule takes effect in this case.

If insurance on the life of an individual is owned by a corporation, and any part of the proceeds is not payable for the benefit of the corporation, any incident of ownership held by the corporation as to part of the proceeds will be attributed to the decedent when he is the sole or the controlling stockholder. If he is the controlling stockholder of a corporation owning a policy on his life, the proceeds of which are payable to his wife, the full proceeds will be included in his estate. If the policy were payable 40 percent to his wife and 60 percent to the corporation, 40 percent of the proceeds would be deemed to be part of his gross estate. An individual is considered a controlling stockholder for this purpose if at the time of his death more than 50 percent of the stock was owned by him and by specified close relatives.

Reversionary interests

If an individual is required by the terms of a divorce decree to name his ex-wife as the beneficiary of certain policies on his life and to keep them in effect for as long as she lives and has not remarried, he has a reversionary interest in the policies. That is, the policies will revert to him should she die or remarry. If his reversionary interest exceeds 5 percent of the value of the property immediately before his death, its entire value is included in his gross estate. If he had provided that upon her death or remarriage the policies would go to a charitable organization and not to him, there would be no reversionary interest and hence no problem.

Simultaneous deaths of spouses

Most states have adopted some version of the Uniform Simultaneous Deaths Act. In these states, if two persons die under circumstances where it isn't possible to determine the order of death, such as in an automobile accident, the insured is presumed to have survived the beneficiary. Anticipate this possibility by naming contingent beneficiaries. If you don't wish to have this order of death apply in the case of simultaneous deaths, the language in your insurance policy or in your will can create other presumptions, such as a reverse-simultaneous-death clause. (See Chapter Seventeen, "Simultaneous Deaths of Spouses.")

Gifts of life insurance

As an individual gets older, he may no longer require so much insurance protection on his life. His older beneficiaries may have died, and his younger ones may now be financially independent. It could be the time to make a gift of policies he owns on his life to his intended beneficiaries. This is a form of gift an individual can make without in anyway impoverishing himself, except to the extent of modest dividends that go to the holders of certain policies. Here is something the donee can't waste. There is no management problem for the financially unsophisticated. If the unified estate and gift credit have been used up, there will be a federal gift tax based on the interpolated terminal reserve of the policy at the time of the gift. You can get this figure from the insurance company that issued the policy, and you must notify the company to make note of the change of ownership. The insurance company will notify the Internal Revenue Service of the transfer and of the value of the interpolated terminal reserve. That means the IRS will automatically be looking for your gift-tax return. Don't disappoint the Service.

Insurance trust

An insurance trust may be used to insulate the policies against claims that may arise from creditors of the insured or of the beneficiaries. The insurance policies are assigned to a fiduciary for the benefit of named parties—the insured no longer owns them. In an unfunded trust, a person transfers policies on his life to a trust and continues to pay the premiums. A funded trust is one in which the grantor not only transfers policies on his life to a trustee but also transfers income-producing properties to provide for the payment of premiums. Another advantage of an insurance trust is that the trustee may be empowered to make the settlement options offered by the policy terms, taking into account facts and circumstances that were not known to the insured when he transferred the policies. This is another technique to allow someone to make discretionary decisions on how the grantor's wealth will be used after his death.

Vulnerability of your insurance to IRS liens

An individual is likely to believe that if major business reverses or uninsured casualties threaten all of his/her other assets, he/she can at least be assured that his/her family will get the proceeds of insurance on his/her life. This may be true with other creditors, but not in the case of the Internal Revenue Service. If a decedent owed the IRS taxes, the Service can attach the cash-surrender value of any policies on his/her life that he/she owned. This extends to policies he/she gave away many years ago if she retained any significant incident of ownership, such as the right to change the name of the beneficiary. If an individual believes the IRS is likely to attach the cash-surrender value of life insurance policies he/she owns, or is deemed to own, he/she should act swiftly to convert the policies to term or some other form that has no cash-surrender value. If his/her finances have made it impossible for him/her to keep up with premium payments, such a conversion may automatically be made by the insurance company. Or the insurance company may use the cash-surrender value to offset the policyholder's indebtedness, acting more rapidly than the IRS.

Conclusions and advice

• Have your tax adviser check the actual policies to see if you have retained any incidents of ownership. You may no longer need them; you may have forgotten you had the powers; you may never have known that your insurance agent retained various rights for you when he/she told the insurance company how to make out various provisions. If you retained the right to repurchase a policy to assigned, that is an incident of ownership.

• Review your insurance program regularly in the light of changed needs of beneficiaries, deaths, and births. Your insurance should be reanalyzed to consider changes in the tax law and significant court decisions.

• Because of your changing age, income, requirements, and beneficiaries' needs, you may find it advisable to exchange some of your policies for other policies more attuned to present circumstances. Check with your tax adviser to find out which policies may be exchanged on a tax-free basis.

• Do not overlook the possibility that inflation will mean that your beneficiaries will require greater inheritances or income from property set aside for their benefit. Additional life insurance may be the only viable way of increasing your assets or estate to make provisions for inflation.

Property owned by one spouse generally passes without estate tax to the surviving spouse under the marital deduction. But when the second spouse dies, to the extent unexpended the survivor's estate will include the value of the property the first spouse had owned. Pay this additional estate tax with the proceeds of "second-to-die" insurance both spouses had taken out and assigned to an insurance trust. As the insurance company has to make only one pay-out, the premium will be much less than if separate policies had been taken out.

• In taking out insurance, a person should consider that statistically the possibility of being disabled from earning a living may be greater than his chance of having an early death.

Chapter Twenty-six

CHOOSING A GOOD RETIREMENT PROGRAM

Your employer's fringe-benefit program can be an important element in your own estate planning. What will be most important to you and your beneficiaries? It might be insurance coverage on your life. It might be an annuity that will also cover the remaining life of your spouse or other designated beneficiaries. It might be some form of wage-continuation plan that could carry to a specified survivor your salary, or a portion of it, for a stipulated length of time after you die. It might be an education fund that could benefit your children. The list is long.

Weigh the available compensation packages

The compensation package of a valued executive or an employee with especially desired skills could be subject to individual negotiation. Consequently, it is important to ascertain what employer-provided benefits would be most desirable in the implementation of your own estate planning and then to bargain from there. It might be advisable to consult with an expert in executive compensation and fringe benefits to learn what kind of package would be most useful to you.

If your employer doesn't offer the type of benefits you would find most desirable for your own estate planning, and if you are unable to negotiate for such an arrangement, consider moving to another employer who will supply what you want. To find out what other employers are providing, it may be necessary to engage an executive-search agency, which should have such information. The fees can be considerable, but they are tax-deductible by an employed executive who is attempting to continue his/her trade or business of being an executive elsewhere.

Desirable compensation plans

Choosing an employer-provided benefit that would be of most value to your own situation and plans necessarily involves consideration of its federal tax impact. Ordinarily the value of anything received as the result of an employer-employee relationship is regarded as additional compensation, taxable as ordinary income. But there are some important exceptions, such as:

1. Group term-life insurance. An employee may exclude from gross income the cost of premiums paid by his employer on group term-life insurance, the excludable cost of which cannot exceed the expense of providing $50,000 of such insurance. The employer's plan to provide group term insurance must not discriminate in favor of key employees as to benefits or type and amount of eligibility. If it does, there is no exclusion for

the premium cost. If an employer pays for the cost of providing coverage in excess of that figure, the additional premiums are taxable income. But the employee couldn't have obtained such coverage at anything like the low premium that the employer pays on a group policy. This treatment is not limited to a lump-sum payment of proceeds upon the death of the insured. The master policy taken out by the employer may provide that payments be made in other ways: For example, the proceeds could go to the employee's beneficiaries in equal annual or monthly installments over a fixed period of time not to exceed 20 years. Or they could be used to purchase a lifetime annuity. The existence of alternative payout options does not affect the plan's status as a tax-favored group term-life insurance policy. Retired employees are treated in the same manner as active employees.

2. Accident and health plans. Premiums paid under an employer's accident and health plan are not includable in gross income. An accident and health plan is an arrangement for payments to employees who are unable to work due to personal injuries or sickness.

3. Medical reimbursement plan. An employee may exclude from gross income any amounts received, directly or indirectly, by himself, his spouse, and his dependents (according to the terms of the plan), as reimbursement for medical expenses if these amounts are attributable to payments made by his employer. This includes payments made directly to physicians and hospitals. A medical reimbursement plan for this purpose cannot discrimi-nate in favor of selected employees—for example, shareholder employees (owners of more than 10 percent of the stock) or highly compensated employees. If the plan does so discriminate, all or part of the reimburse-ment becomes taxable compensation to the selected employees. For example,

a plan is discriminatory if benefits are in proportion to employee compensation, for in that case benefits to top personnel will be higher. The employee is clearly better off with tax-free reimbursement under a qualified plan, since only medical expenses exceeding 7½ percent of his adjusted gross income can be deducted on his federal income-tax return.

4. Group legal-service plan. Excludable from an employee's gross income are (a) amounts contributed by an employer to a qualified group legal-service plan for employees (and their spouses and dependents, if covered) and (b) any personal legal services received by an employee or any amounts reimbursed to him under such a plan for legal services for him, his spouse, and his dependents. The benefits must be provided on a nondiscriminatory basis, although presumably highly compensated persons will get involved in more business or investment situations requiring legal services. The plan must be organized through insurance companies or qualified tax-free organizations and trusts. Not more than 25 percent of the amounts contributed by an employer in any single year may be provided for employees (or their spouses or dependents) who own more than a 5 percent interest in the company. Employers now may use any nondiscriminatory definition of compensation. This exclusion was scheduled to expire as to taxable years beginning after September 30, 1990.

Tax-favored benefits

Consider other employer plans in the light of your own estate-planning objectives. Even if employer-financed benefits of a particular type are taxable, an employee can still reap a substantial benefit from them. For example, if the employee is in a 45 percent income-tax bracket, only 55 percent of the employer's cost in providing the benefits will be effectively taxed.

The employer may provide very desirable status symbols as a non-monetary (and non-taxable) benefit. Examples: a highly prized office location and an "executive" assistant.

Here are some additional employer-provided benefits that should be helpful in individual estate planning:

• Life insurance. Many employers participate with employees in securing insurance on the employees' lives. (See Chapter Twenty-seven, "Split-Dollar Insurance.")

• Scholarships. Many corporations make scholarships available to children of employees. In other instances, executives or stockholders of a corporation set up scholarship funds for the use of needy persons, with first preference given to the children of present or past employees. Your children might meet the necessary standards of eligibility.

• Education trusts. A corporation may set up a trust to pay for college or other defined educational expenses of designated key employees. If an employee has several children and the available coverage is less than the trust provides, the employee may choose which child will be covered; if that child leaves college or otherwise becomes ineligible, the employee may name a "replacement" child. There is no taxable income to the employee until payouts are made for the benefit of his children.

• Retirement plans. The employer corporation may have a pension or deferred-profit-sharing plan that provides retirement benefits for employees. In some instances, the spouses or other relatives of the employees may benefit from them as well. (See Chapter Twenty-eight, "Tax-Favored Retirement Benefits.")

• Annuities. The employer may provide a retirement annuity for an employee, or a survivorship annuity covering the employee and his spouse or other beneficiary. (See Chapter Thirty-two, "Annuities.")

• Deferred compensation. Advantageous arrangements may be made with an employer to have a certain portion of the employee's compensation payable after a specified number of years, which may be after the employee retires and is presumably in a lower tax bracket. (See Chapter Twenty-nine, "Deferred-Compensation Arrangements.")

• Interest-free loans. Although most economic advantages obtained as the result of an employer-employee relationship are taxed as additional compensation (why else were they paid?), this is not the case with interest-free loans except in a few isolated situations that most individuals will never encounter. When interest rates soar, free interest is an attractive fringe benefit. Find out what the employer's policy is in providing this benefit.

• Stock options and stock-purchase plans. These are complex subjects that should be discussed with your tax adviser. Incentive stock options now provide substantial tax benefits as well as increasing your chance to own part of the business. Before entering upon a stock-option plan, find out whether it qualifies for tax benefits and what the conditions are in the event of your death. For example, will exercising the option make you subject to the alternative minimum tax? Will the option granted to you be exercisable by your spouse if you die before exercising it? If you purchase stock in a closely-held corporation, will your executors have to sell it back to the corporation at the time of your death under a formula or at a price that might be undesirable, such as original cost? Is the stock subject to a buy-sell agreement? (See Chapter Twenty-two, "Buy-Sell Agreements.")

• Directors' and officers' liability insurance. Such premiums, although paid by the employer corporation, are not regarded as income taxable to the employee. The existence of such a policy could save an individual or an estate a considerable amount of expense in the event of an unfortunate business decision or act.

• Extended working period. If that is what you desire, will your employer permit you to work beyond the company's stated mandatory retirement age? Will employer-provided fringe benefits be added to your compensation after normal retirement age? Can you get assurance that you'll be retained as a part-time consultant after you retire?

Conclusions and advice

• Keep abreast of changes in your employer's benefit package. Check your own objectives regularly. Your economic circumstances, as well as the employer corporation's executives, vary from time to time.

• Find out if an employer fringe-benefit plan is discriminatory. If it is, all tax benefits to you may be lost even though you had nothing to do with the discriminatory practice.

• Executive-search-agency fees and moving expenses are deductible in many instances. Check with tax counsel to find out whether your costs in finding and accepting employment with a corporation that has more attractive fringe benefits are deductible for income-tax purposes.

• Do not assume that higher salary must be the most desirable form of compensation. Consider the after-tax effects.

• Do not assume that all group insurance premiums are excludable from gross income for up to $50,000 of coverage. This refers only to group term-life insurance.

• Do not assume that all corporate compensation packages are the same. Have you shopped around recently? Have you tried to negotiate for a compensation arrangement appropriate to your own needs?

• If an employee is covered by certain kinds of retirement plans, he can choose to have part of his compensation contributed by his employer to a retirement fund rather than paid to him. These amounts are called elective deferrals, because he may choose (elect) to set aside the money and defer the income tax on the amount until it is distributed to him. These elective deferrals include deferred contributions to cash or deferral arrangements (known as Section 401(k) plans). Because these contributions are considered to be made by the employer, the employee is taxed on any payments he receives from the retirement fund unless he rolls over the payments. (For an explanation of this, speak to your tax adviser; or see IRS Publication 575, pages 25–29.) In general, an employee may not defer more than a total of $8,994 for all qualified plans by which he is covered. This limit may be subject to annual increases to reflect inflation, as measured by the Consumer Price Index.

• An employment contract providing that the employer will pay benefits to an employee's spouse in the event he dies while still on the payroll has become much more attractive. In 1992 the IRS reversed its prior position and now holds that this is not to be treated as a taxable gift to her.

Chapter Twenty-seven

SPLIT-DOLLAR INSURANCE

Under the procedure for split-dollar life insurance, employer and employee join in purchasing an insurance contract, in which there is a substantial investment element, on the life of the employee. The employer provides the funds to pay that part of the annual premium equal to the increase in the cash-surrender value each year, and the employee pays the balance of the annual premium.

When the employee dies, the employer is entitled to receive, out of the proceeds of the policy, an amount equal to the cash-surrender value, or at least a sufficient part of it to equal the funds it has provided for the premium payments. The employee has the right to name the beneficiary of the balance of any proceeds payable by reason of his/her death. In practical effect, although the employee must pay a substantial part of the first premium, after the first year his/her share of the premium decreases rapidly, and in some cases it even becomes zero after a relatively few years. The employee thus obtains valuable insurance protection (decreasing each year, but still substantial for a long time) with a relatively small outlay for premiums in the early years, and at little or no cost to him/her in later years.

Forms of split-dollar life insurance

Two major types of split-dollar arrangements are in use: the endorsement system and the collateral-assignment system. In the endorsement system, the employer owns the policy and is responsible for payment of the annual premiums. The employee is then required to reimburse the employer for his/her share, if any, of the premiums. Under the collateral assignment system, the employee in form owns the policy and pays the entire premium on it. The employer in form makes annual loans to the employee, without interest or below the going rate, of amounts equal to the yearly increase in cash-surrender value, but not exceeding the annual premium. The employee executes an assignment of his/her policy to the employer as collateral for the loans. The loans are generally payable at the termination of employment or on the death of the employee.

Income-tax treatment

The employee receives an economic benefit represented by the amount of annual premium cost that he/she is relieved of paying and would otherwise have to bear in the absence of this arrangement. The amount to be included in the employee's gross income each year is an amount equal to the one-year cost of declining life insurance protection to which he/she is entitled from year to year, less the portion—if any—that he/she pays for.

Under some arrangements, current insurance protection is not the only benefit an employee receives. He may receive others, as well, such as cash dividends on the policy or additional life insurance. If the policyholder dividend is distributed to him, the amount of the dividend must be aggregated with the other benefits he receives under the arrangement for the purpose of determining the amount includable in his gross income. Similarly, if the dividend is used to purchase additional one-year term insurance for the employee, or paid-up life insurance (in which he has a nonforfeitable interest) for a period of more than one year, he receives an additional economic benefit, the value of which is equal to the amount of the dividend. When the dividend is used to purchase additional paid-up life insurance for a period of more than one year, and the employer retains the right to the cash-surrender value of this additional insurance, the annual value of the additional insurance coverage is includable in the employee's gross income. The value of the benefit to be included each year may be determined in that manner.

According to a 1978 ruling by the Internal Revenue Service, the split-dollar tax treatment rules apply when the owner of the policy is not an employee but someone else selected by him/her.

Deductibility

Neither the employer nor the employee is entitled to a tax deduction for premiums on split-dollar life insurance. As far as the employer is concerned, he/she will get back the cost of the policy when it is ultimately paid off on the employee's death. In effect, this is a loan by the employer without interest, or at low interest, and it does not represent taxable income to the employee. The employee receives most of the protection under such an arrangement, but he/she pays only a small part of the cost.

Conclusions and advice

• When discussing a position with a potential new employer, find out whether there is a split-dollar insurance plan. This can provide insurance that the employee might not be able to afford, or coverage financed in part by the employer.

• Since this procedure is not widely known, bring it to the attention of your employer if he/she doesn't have such a plan.

• Because of the role played by cash-surrender value in determining the premium paid each year by employer and employee, do not use a form of life insurance that lacks a substantial investment element.

• Do not seek to deduct any part of the cost in filing your tax returns.

Chapter Twenty-eight

TAX-FAVORED
RETIREMENT BENEFITS

An individual derives several advantages from a retirement program financed entirely or in large measure by an employer. Chief among them:

1. Although it is a general principle of the tax law that an employee is taxed upon the value of any economic benefit derived as a result of the employer-employee relationship, in the case of a qualified retirement program (that is, one approved by the Internal Revenue Service), the individual isn't taxed until she/he receives payment. Her/his income is almost invariably lower after retirement than when she/he is still on salary, so that the tax impact is lower than if she/he were taxed each year on the increment of what accrues.

2. The employer, within limits set by the tax law, is entitled to immediate tax deductions.

3. The trust that is used to administer most qualified retirement

plans is set up on a tax-exempt basis for the benefit of employees or their beneficiaries. Consequently, any accumulations of income or capital through interest, dividends, rents, capital gains, and the like are tax-free. An individual who accumulates money for his/her own retirement would not have comparable tax-exempt accumulation.

In addition, the employee has an involuntary savings program. She/he will not have to rely only on her/his own capital to see her/him through the retirement years, because government restrictions and regulations imposed on such plans and their administrators ensure that planned benefits are delivered. This security permits the employee to make dispositions of her other property, reducing what would be her/his gross estate when she/he dies.

Pension or deferred-profit-sharing plan?

The two most popular types of employer-financed retirement programs are the pension plan (also known as a defined-benefits plan) and the deferred-profit-sharing plan (also known as a defined-contributions plan). Although each can have provisions for earlier payouts, as in the case of permanent disability, most plans provide benefits at retirement. Reduced payments may be permitted for retirement a few years before the standard targeted retirement age.

It is customarily the employer's decision which type of retirement plan she/he will provide. Employee choices, if the plan so provides, are:

• Whether to retire at, before, or after the company's normal retirement date.

• Whether to participate if the plan is of the contributory type.

- Whether to take a payout in the form of an annuity or as a lump-sum payment where the plan allows this choice.

- Whether to take a retirement annuity in the form of a single-life contract for the employee or a survivorship annuity that covers the employee and another designated party, most frequently a spouse.

Plans must provide survivorship coverage for spouses and an employee must affirmatively act to avoid such coverage if she/he is married. But an individual has a more basic decision as to the form of employer retirement program that will apply to her/him. She/he can select an employer on the basis of the latter's retirement-program provisions. Of vital concern are whether the employer has a pension or a deferred-profit-sharing plan (few have both), the coverage requirements (how long one has to work before becoming qualified under the program), the vesting requirements (what monetary rights accumulate for the individual after specified periods that can't be lost through resignation or dismissal), the possibility of obtaining benefits in a lump sum, the opportunity to transfer accrued benefits to another retirement program without present tax consequences (a rollover), early-retirement provisions, and what happens if an employee wants to continue working after the stated retirement date. Usually one doesn't regard a company's retirement program as a major factor in choosing an employer or in changing jobs. But that choice has a definite impact on an estate plan. If an employer has a good retirement program, plus a generous medical reimbursement and health plan, the employee is not obliged to retain as much capital to deal with these expenses on her/his own.

Qualified pension plans

Pension plans are covered by the strict requirements of the Pension Reform Act of 1974 if the employer does business in interstate commerce. Some other employers, as a competitive measure, have voluntarily adopted plans to meet these rules. A well-informed employee may choose not to take a job with a company that has a nonqualified pension plan—that is, one that doesn't meet the ground rules for companies engaged in interstate commerce. Such a plan provides little assurance that the benefits won't go disproportionately to a few favored persons, that the employee will not lose all of the pension rights that have been building up over the years if he/she is discharged before retirement or decides to work elsewhere, that the money will really be there when he/she retires, that she won't have to wait an unreasonably long time to get retirement benefits, and that her/his financial involvement in the plan will not be treated by the employer as something he/she has no right to know about or question.

Coverage

If a corporation has a qualified retirement plan, the federal tax law defines the minimum percentage of employees who must be covered—that is, benefited by the plan. Certain employees may be excluded by the terms of a plan, such as those who have worked for the employer for less than a specified length of time or those who work on a part-time or seasonal basis.

The technical requirements of a plan ensuring that available tax advantages for both employer and employee are available involve areas over which an employee has no control. There are intricate rules governing the failure of a plan to qualify because of inadequate coverage of the work force, discrimination in favor of highly compensated employees, reduction of benefits because of early retirement, rollovers of an employee's accrued benefits under the plan when she/he changes employment, and tax treatment of a lump-sum distribution of accrued benefits instead of annual payments. An employee may be able to learn these details from a designated representative of the employer. Whether the employer actually complies with the highly technical requirements of the law, so that employee benefits really are being safeguarded, is usually something an employee has no way of knowing.

Vesting

Vesting is the irrevocable transfer of the employer's contributions to the retirement fund to the credit of an employee. Various alternatives are available for a qualified plan's provision as to when employee rights become vested. But each covered employee's rights must be fully vested when she/he reaches the normal or stated retirement age, or when she/he actually retires.

Discrimination

A qualified retirement plan must not discriminate in favor of officers, employee stockholders, or other highly compensated employees, either in the actual language of the plan or the way in which it operates.

The tax law defines what is meant by the term "highly compensated."

Past-service credit

A current pension plan makes provision for retirement benefits based upon salaries for the number of years of coverage under the plan. But an individual may have worked for the company for many years before the plan was adopted. If it so chooses, a corporation may adopt a past-service-credit plan. Employees, in addition to credits based upon current service, may be given credits for the number of years, or for a specified number of those years, before the plan went into effect. This can make a considerable difference in the amount of pension benefits available to an employee who worked for the company prior to the time it adopted its pension plan.

Benefits

Under a pension plan (defined-benefit plan), an employee must be able to ascertain what he/she will actually receive upon retirement at the specified time; but he/she must assume how many years he/she will work and what his/her compensation will be during his/her remaining years of employment. It is up to the employer to provide the financial means each year, so that when an individual does retire, his/her benefits will be there. This usually requires elaborate computations by an actuary. In order to make certain that the employer does have the funds in hand, the tax law provides strict penalties for noncompliance.

If the pension plan is underfunded

If an employee becomes entitled to retirement benefits under a qualified pension plan, and the implementing trust or fund lacks the money to honor this commitment, the Pension Benefit Guarantee Corporation, a federal agency, steps in. This corporation is funded by premiums paid by each covered employer. When a corporation's pension fund can't make the required payments because the plan has been underfunded and Pension Benefit Guarantee Corporation moneys are used for this purpose, that agency can recover from the employer amounts up to 30 percent of the company's net worth. In certain situations, an employer might have two or more qualified pension plans, covering different types of employees or functions. Underfunding could subject the employer to reimbursement payments to the Guarantee Corporation of up to 30 percent of net worth for each such plan. The same penalty applies to a corporation with a defunct subsidiary whose plan was underfunded.

Retirement annuities

When a plan provides for a retirement benefit in the form of an annuity, and the employee has been married for the one-year period ending on the annuity starting date, the plan must provide for a joint and survivor annuity with the employee's spouse. This annuity must be for not less than half of the annuity payable to the participant during the joint lives of the participant and her/his spouse. But the employee may elect to receive the higher return of a single-life annuity if the spouse consents. The employer must supply the necessary figures so that the employee can have before him/her the computations for both bases. The time for supplying this information varies according to certain specified circumstances. For example, in the case of an employee who leaves his/her place of employment before age 35, distributions after December 31, 1989, must be made within "a reasonable time."

Protection against mergers

A qualified pension plan must provide protection to participants in the case of a merger of the plan with another plan or the transfer of assets or liabilities from a plan. The value of benefits to the participant and the extent to which the benefits have been funded is protected by comparing what the benefits would have been if the plan had terminated immediately before the merger and what they would be under the plan had it terminated just after the merger. The postmerger termination benefit may not be less than the premerger termination benefit.

Termination of employment

Somehow, consideration of the advantages of pension plans always assumes that the employee will get back more than she/he puts into the fund. It doesn't always work out that way, however. If she/he gets back less than she/he paid in under a contributory plan, for example, because the fund's investments have been unsuccessful, she/he can deduct the difference as an ordinary loss in the year of the lump-sum distribution to her/him.

If an employee's services are terminated, she/he is likely to have accrued benefits. Any payments she/he receives will constitute taxable income to her/him. In addition, the accumulation of amounts established to her/his credit in the fund will no longer be on a tax-free basis if she/he withdraws them from the tax-exempt trust. But the employee may be able to avoid present tax impact when she/he withdraws from coverage under a qualified pension plan; if she/he receives the money as a lump-sum payment, she/he may transfer it to an Individual Retirement Account (IRA) or to the qualified pension plan trust of a new employer if that employer agrees, as long as she/he does so within 60 days. Such a tax-free rollover can be used only once every three years.

Penalties

Penalties are imposed on the trustees of a qualified pension plan if it violates the strict requirements of the law. The only impact of this upon the employee is that it tends to ensure that the plan and its implementing fund or trust will be supervised very carefully. On the other hand, rather than face penalties, management may decide that it doesn't want to have a qualified pension plan at all; and this definitely affects the employees.

Deferred-profit-sharing plans

Because of a corporation's vulnerability to a levy of up to 30 percent of net worth in the case of an underfunded plan, plus the personal liabilities in which executives or plan trustees can be involved, many corporations have become disenchanted with qualified pension plans. Instead, they may adopt a deferred-profit-sharing plan to provide employee retirement benefits. Such plans are less "dangerous" because there are no minimum funding requirements and no harsh financial consequences in case of underfunding.

The employer may take a specified percentage of its profits each year as a deduction by paying it into its qualified-profit-sharing plan (defined-contributions plan). The portion of employer profits to be shared with employees that exceeds this specified percentage in any year is an unallowable deduction, which may be carried forward by the employer for use in future years when the deduction would otherwise be less than the specified percentage.

A deferred-profit-sharing plan may provide for the payment of amounts into a fund for ultimate payout to eligible participants. The difference between this and a pension plan is that under the latter, retirement benefits are the amounts called for by the plan itself, subject only to the number of years of coverage and the amount of compensation on which benefits are based. The deferred-profit-sharing plan, on the other hand, guarantees no specific amount. Even assuming that the funds are available when employees become entitled to them, the amounts available depend upon corporate profits. And there is, of course, no way of determining what these profits will be in future years.

"Profits" may be anything defined by the plan itself, for example—book profits, book profits with certain specified adjustments, income exclusive of capital gains, income exclusive of revenues from foreign operations, income as calculated on the federal income-tax return. The portion of defined income that is to be shared with the employees via the deferred profit-sharing plan should also be specified—for example, 50 percent of income above $100,000, or a sliding scale of percentages of corporate income.

Payouts

An employee entitled to deferred-profit-sharing-plan benefits may receive payment under a unit system. For example, employees' shares may be determined by assigning units for compensation, length of service, and age. An employee's share of the employer contribution is that proportion of the entire amount that the number of units assigned to her/him bears to the total number of units assigned to all employees. In working out the allocation, units are given a dollar value by dividing the total number issued into the total employer contribution.

In this case, unlike that of a qualified pension plan, an employee gains from the departure of other employees to the extent their interests have not vested. Amounts forfeited by reason of employees' premature departure become available as part of the total to be shared by the remaining employees. By contrast, the rights of an employee who is covered by a qualified pension plan don't change, regardless of what happens to other employees or their shares in a retirement program.

What type of plan is better for you

It cannot be stated categorically whether an employee benefits more from the existence of a qualified pension plan or a deferred-profit-sharing plan. There is certainly far more assurance of getting retirement benefits under a qualified pension plan.

The actual benefits, however, could be far more or less under a deferred-profit-sharing plan, depending upon the profit-sharing arrangement, the profits over the years, and the number of employees whose interests are forfeited in favor of the remaining employees. A qualified pension plan may provide for past-service credits, an unusual arrangement for deferred-profit-sharing plans.

There has been some criticism, chiefly from labor unions, that corporations offering deferred-profit-sharing plans may conceal earnings so that they don't have to be shared with the rank-and-file employees. But a deferred-profit-sharing plan offers this advantage:

Employees are apt to work harder, and to see that unnecessary expenses and waste are eliminated or at least reduced, if they realize that they will share in any additional profits resulting from increased dedication to their jobs.

Qualified-benefit-plan exclusion

In the case of decedents who died after December 31, 1984, there no longer exists a previous $100,000 limitation on the estate-tax exclusions for retirement benefits under qualified pension plans, tax-sheltered annuities, individual retirement arrangements, and certain military retirement plans.

Top-heavy plans

As of 1984, special new rules apply to "top-heavy" plans—those whose benefits flow to a limited number of shareholders, partners, or key employees. Such plans must provide for faster vesting for nonkey employees, and minimum benefits or contributions are required for such nonkey employees.

The plans won't be able to take Social Security benefits and contributions into account in determining these minimum benefits or contributions. These new rules apply to both corporate plans and Keogh-type plans for the self-employed.

Conclusions and advice

• Have an expert in the field compare the pension plans of corporations where you are considering securing employment.

• Insist on an understandable explanation of your corporation's qualified pension plan as required by law.

• Do not rely on today's indicated pension payouts. The corporation may obtain permission from the Internal Revenue Service to discontinue its plan, for example, because of circumstances that could not reasonably have been foreseen when the plan was adopted. You may have vested rights, but only to accrued benefits and not to the future.

• The economic climate or a major corporate "restructuring" may mean that the stated plan benefits will shrink or even disappear entirely.

• If a company for which the decendent had worked has gone out of business, the executor should write to the Pension Benefit Guaranty Corporation, Missing Participant Program, 1200 K Street NW, Washington, DC 20005. This program seeks to locate plans that have been terminated, or taken over by the agency. The letter should include the name, address, telephone number, Social Security number, date of birth, name and location of the employer, and any documents issued by the plan.

• Do not rely on the permanency of the language in the present version of the tax law. It could be changed at any time by a volatile Congress, as in the case of various tax-favored treatments.

Chapter Twenty-nine

DEFERRED-COMPENSATION ARRANGEMENTS

Financially, an individual may be doing very well today—but tomorrow, when he retires or when his income tapers off due to health reasons or lessened activities, could be another matter. If he retains his assets so that he can live after retirement or with shortened workdays on the income that is produced by these assets, his gross estate at death will be larger than it needs to be. In addition, he won't have the satisfaction of giving properties to his beneficiaries while he is still alive. And in those later years, he may no longer have the capacity to administer or retain his assets properly.

With careful planning, however, this individual can arrange now to have some of the income he doesn't need today deferred until later years. At that time, it might be taxed at lower rates because he no longer has his salary or his business income.

Nature of deferred income

Pension and deferred-profit-sharing plans are forms of deferred compensation. (See Chapter Twenty-eight, "Tax-Favored Retirement Benefits.") Here are some others:

Ordinarily, when someone earns income in a particular year, regardless of when he or somebody else actually receives the payments, it is taxable in that year if he could have gotten the money without any substantial restrictions or difficulty. This is called "constructive receipt of income." For example, savings-bank interest is taxed in the year earned, even if the depositor never bothered to withdraw it or have it entered in his passbook. But an individual hasn't received income if there is substantial question as to whether he will ever receive it. There may be a provision that income earned today will be paid to the employee in 10 years, or at the time he retires, if he has not gone into competition with his employer corporation. Until the specified time of payment, however, it isn't known whether he has honored the commitment. In other words, he has no taxable income until it is established whether he has gone into competition against the corporation.

Another arrangement may call for part of the income that a person earns today to be paid to him in yearly or other installments until he dies, provided he holds himself available for consultations if requested by the corporation. Only on a year-to-year basis can it be determined whether he has done so, a fact not affected by whether the employer ever asks his advice. The possibility exists that he could forfeit his right to receive the deferred compensation, so he isn't taxed on it until payment is made by reason of the fact that the forfeiture provisions were not triggered.

Unfunded compensation—a danger

An element of risk to the employee is involved in a deferred-compensation arrangement where the money is not actually safeguarded for future payouts to the employee by being deposited in a trust fund for his benefit or in an escrow account in his name. The risk is that when the time for scheduled payment arrives, the employer simply won't have the funds to honor it. So if the deferred-compensation plan is not funded, and the employee takes the risk that he might never be paid, the income goes untaxed until the year or years when he actually receives it.

If there is no forfeiture provision that could cause the employee to lose his right to future payment, and if there is a trust or other arrangement that assures him that the money is there waiting for the payout date, he is taxed in the year his services are performed. But under one procedure, an employee can be assured that the money will be there. One employee was granted a deferred-compensation arrangement by his employer, the agreement to run until he reached age 65 or his employment was terminated. The employer purchased an annuity contract to fund its deferred-compensation liability. The annuity contract was owned by the corporation, which was the beneficiary, and the contract was subject to claims of the corporation's general creditors. The employee was taxed only when he received the deferred payments, for he had no interest in the annuity. But he had reason to be confident that he would get his money when it was due—unless the corporation's creditors got there first.

Taxability

A deferred-compensation plan postpones taxability until the payment date if the election to defer income is made before the period in which the services are to be rendered. In one instance, a contract provided that each year officers could, before income for the following year was earned, elect irrevocably to defer receipt of specified portions of their salaries, which would then be paid ratably over a 10-year period. A deferred-compensation account was set up on the corporate books for each officer who made the election, but the amounts thus deferred were to be satisfied only from general corporate funds, which could have been subjected to creditors' claims. The amounts deferred were not taxable to electing officers in the year earned but in the years received.

Key to a contract

In another situation, an employee and a corporation executed a five-year employment contract providing for a stated annual salary and a stipulated amount of additional compensation. The additional compensation was to be credited to a bookkeeping reserve account, to be deferred, accumulated, and paid in annual installments equal to one-fifth of the amount in reserve as of the close of the year immediately preceding the year of the corporation's payment. Payments were to begin only when the individual (a) terminated full-time employment, (b) became a part-time employee of the corporation, or (c) became partially or totally incapacitated. The corporation was merely under a contractual obligation; there was no trust arrangement to ensure that the employee would in fact get the money.

The contract provided that if the employee should fail or refuse to perform his duties, the corporation would be relieved of its obligation to make any further credits to the reserve. It also provided that, should he die prior to his receipt in full of the balance in the account, the remaining balance would be payable to any party he named at the rate of one-fifth per year for five years. The Internal Revenue Service ruled that the additional compensation stipulated under the contract would be taxable to the employee only in the years he actually received installment payments in cash from the amounts credited to his account.

Spurs to performance

Another corporation set up a supplementary retirement plan under which a committee of directors (none of whom was an officer or employee) could award incentive bonuses to selected employees for payment at future dates to be designated by that employee. Employees thus tapped had no right to any money until the date they named, and no payment could be made more than 10 years after an employee's normal retirement date. The awards were not funded, nor could they be assigned, although they would be paid to the employee's beneficiary at the time of his death.

Federal estate tax

Federal estate-tax problems may arise in the case of a deferred-compensation arrangement. In one case, a corporation agreed to make specified payments to an employee on his retirement or to his nominee if he died. There were certain forfeiture provisions, but all possibilities of forfeiture ended with the employee's death. The value of the payments the corporation was obliged to make to his nominee after his death was included in his gross estate.

But nothing was includable in the gross estate of one executive who, with four others, was covered by an agreement under which the employer corporation undertook to pay specified annuities to the widows of any executives who died while still employed. Here the contract identified each wife by name. The husband never had any right to the annuity or any property interest in it. He couldn't alter it or change the name of the beneficiary, for the agreement's parties were only the corporation and an executive's wife as an individual.

Interplay with economic factors

An executive should consider the merits of a deferred-compensation plan carefully. As the dollar deteriorates in value, the employee might prefer to take his money today rather than at a time when it will be worth less. If the deferred compensation is not set aside in the individual's name (as in a trust fund), there is a possibility that because of poor business conditions the money will not be paid when it is due. Mounting economic pressures might result in higher tax rates when the individual retires than at present, even if his income is less.

Conclusions and advice

• Make the arrangement before income is actually earned.

• If income is to be paid to a nominee after the executive's death, specify several persons, such as children or grandchildren, so that the tax impact on the payees will be less.

• Consider using a deferred-compensation arrangement for someone who seems unable to invest unneeded current income wisely.

• Do not agree to such an arrangement with a corporation that is of questionable financial stature, for with all the good faith in the world, the commitment may not be honored.

- Do not make an arrangement where income is earned currently and the deferral amounts to constructive receipt of income that is merely made payable in the future for the convenience of the employee. If the income is really subject to his command, it is not deferred compensation.

- Beware of financial, personnel, policy, or other changes that will imperil your future benefits.

Chapter Thirty

HOW TO GET MORE LIFE INSURANCE

Among those who suffer most from the economic effects of inflation is the mature executive who once took out insurance on his life in an amount that was generous in terms of his earnings and his estate-planning objectives at the time. When his policies matured at his death, the proceeds would provide for his spouse or other beneficiaries to the extent he had decided upon.

But his planning was done long ago, based upon medical expenses and other costs of the past. Now that severe inflation has set in, his estate plans must be revised.

Inflation calls for more insurance. Can you still get it?

How is it possible to refinance an estate plan at this time? The classic solution to the problem of how to increase one's estate when income and the stock market won't do the job is to take out additional insurance on one's life. But our businessman is now middle-aged. The cost of additional insurance starting at his present age would be tremendous. Even more seriously, he may now be uninsurable. His business success may also have accustomed him to a standard of living that he doesn't want to lower too drastically.

Life insurance without the necessity of taking a physical examination is the best possibility. If it is group insurance, the costs are appreciably less than would be the case if the employee took out his own individual policy. If the coverage is group term-life, there is the important advantage of not having to report as income the premiums paid by his employer on the cost of providing up to $50,000 in coverage provided the plan doesn't discriminate. (See Chapter Twenty-six, "Choosing a Good Retirement Program.")

A new employer can mean new insurance

The solution, then, is to locate an employer that has a liberal group term-life insurance program for its employees. The best possibility for our aging executive who wants to move is to sign up with an executive-search agency, the sizable fees of which are tax-deductible in most instances. If, in your preliminary interview, you ascertain that this agency hasn't done its homework in analyzing compensation packages well enough to know about the group insurance plans available from various employers, you should look elsewhere.

There are many factors the executive should consider before moving to a corporation because it has a good group term-insurance program. He

190

will have to learn about the pension or deferred-profit-sharing plan, especially those provisions on minimum number of years (if any) before coverage and the rapidity of vesting. (See Chapter Twenty-eight, "Tax-Favored Retirement Benefits.") Ask your executive-search agency about corporations that offer the rather recent "cafeteria plans" (discussed in Chapter Twenty-six), which allow an employee to "shop around" for benefits. If group term insurance is one of the benefits in a cafeteria plan, work at such a corporation offers annual reelection of the particular fringe benefits desired, giving the employee a degree of flexibility.

Conversion privilege

If an executive leaves a corporation with a group insurance plan to work for a corporation with an appreciably less liberal plan, before leaving he should find out whether there is a conversion privilege. Some plans have provisions for someone who leaves a group insurance program to convert his group policy to an individual one, with identical coverage, often without physical examination, at the prevailing rate for individual insurance at the date of conversion. That could be costly. But the executive might well also regard it as indispensable—the only method of increasing his insurance coverage.

Conclusions and advice

• Find out from an authoritative source what employer-corporation group-insurance programs are available in liberal amounts before leaving your present job. Usually this means engaging an executive-search agency. Fees paid to such an agency are deductible if you are still employed at the time you pay the fee. Expenses related to employment are in general deductible. If you are an executive when you pay the fee, this is a payment in connection with your business of being an executive.

• Question the possibility of converting your group insurance to individual policies before accepting employment with another company.

• Do not consider group insurance as the sole reason for making a change of employment. But it can be an extremely important reason.

Chapter Thirty-one

SPOUSE INSURANCE

Most men are aware of the importance of taking out a sizable amount of insurance on their lives to protect their wives and children. But they might neglect something that's just as important: taking out life insurance for a wife to provide financial reimbursement for the amount of loss that would result from her death.

Tax cost of losing a spouse

Apart from a number of heavy incidental costs (including those of the funeral), there are tax reasons for taking out such insurance. In most situations, federal income tax is lower when a married couple files a joint return. The most extreme example occurs when one spouse has substantially all of the income.

The differences would be less spectacular if both spouses had an income, especially if these incomes were about the same. In this case, there is usually a tax advantage in not being married. Most often, there is a distinct tax advantage if an individual with a sizable income, such as a business executive, files a joint return with someone who has a smaller income, such as his nonworking spouse.

There are, however, some disadvantages to filing a joint return. An executor might want to consider forgoing a joint return, since each party to a joint return can ordinarily be held liable for any tax deficiency, regardless of which party failed to report income. If the survivor was the spouse with the larger income, he will have additional taxes to pay, for the savings resulting from the filing of joint returns have been forfeited. That there is additional tax is not of so much concern to the executor as seeing that his/her client, the decedent, is not charged with income that the survivor might have omitted from the return, as would happen on a joint return.

In the case of the federal estate tax, loss of one's spouse can result in a major tax disadvantage. The largest deduction from gross estate in the case of married couples is generally the marital deduction. (See Chapter Fourteen, "The Marital Deduction.") If there is no surviving spouse to whom property can pass, there is no marital deduction.

The death of a spouse can result in federal estate tax in the case of jointly owned property. The tax law automatically assumes that half of this property was owned by the co-owner who died first. So half the value of property owned by husband and wife will be includable in the gross estate of the first spouse to die. And the surviving spouse will get stepped-up basis only for that half of the property.

The gift-tax marital deduction is also lost upon the death of a spouse to the extent that it was not previously utilized. Obviously the advantage of gift-splitting by the spouses is no longer possible after one of them dies.

Other expenses and costs after death of one spouse

The death of a spouse can mean financial stress for the survivor. A nonearning spouse might have to face a considerable drop in his/her standard of living; a working parent with a young family would have to pay someone to look after the household and the children.

The solution

Assuming that the surviving spouse has the additional net tax expense and higher costs resulting from the death of the other, spouse insurance is clearly indicated, in addition to insurance taken out for other reasons or purposes.

Conclusions and advice

• Make projections of the tax and other continuing expenses you would have should your spouse die before you do. This will indicate the amount of spouse insurance you will require solely for reimbursement purposes.

• If certain of these expenses and costs will be lower as the children grow up or other circumstances change, consider taking out declining-balance term insurance.

• Do not take for granted the likelihood that your spouse will outlive you simply because he/she is younger or in better health.

- "Second to die" insurance can be taken out to provide for this problem; because of the so-called unlimited marital deduction, or by reason of gifts or other transfers, property that one spouse (here called the husband for convenience) had owned will not be taxed to his estate if he dies before his wife does. But when the second spouse (here referred to as the wife) dies, her estate will now include both her own property and what escaped her husband's estate tax because it was no longer his. That, in effect, can mean a doubled or at least a greatly higher estate tax when she dies. Provide for this with survivorship insurance, payable when the second spouse dies. The federal estate tax is payable nine months after a decedent's death, and the tax on the combined assets of both estates (less the value of property meanwhile consumed) could be too large an amount to be paid by the executors of the wife's estate. The result: Without this insurance, estate assets might have to be liquidated at an unfortunate time. The premiums on "second to die" insurance are generally much lower than those on individual life policies because the insurance company does not have to pay off the face value of the policy until the second spouse dies.

Chapter Thirty-two

ANNUITIES

An annuity is generally a fixed payment, made either in a lump sum or periodically. It is usually in the form of a promise to pay an individual a fixed monthly sum for life. The cost of purchasing an annuity depends on the number and amount of payments and the life expectancy of the annuitant. The amount to be paid out is more than the purchase price; this reflects the fact that the present value of a dollar to be paid now is more than the value will be in a few years, because the seller of the annuity has had the use of the money for those years.

Life expectancies are established by actuarial studies of the population as a whole, not by individual experience. The annuity owner who lives longer than the actuarial average, therefore, may receive quite a bit more money than he/she was led to expect. In other words, the purchaser of a commercial periodic annuity (one bought from an insurance company, for example) is guaranteed an income he/she cannot outlive.

An annuity can cut down the expense and delay of probating a will and its dispositions. It enables the owner, or annuitant, to plan on giving away portions of his wealth, reducing what will be his ultimate gross estate. And if the property he gives away is of an income-producing nature, he will also reduce current income taxes.

The purchaser of a commercial annuity has a high degree of assurance that he will not dissipate the capital needed for his last years by poor judgment. On the other hand, the real value of the annuity may be severely eroded by inflation.

Variable annuities

As noted, most annuities are paid out in fixed annual or periodic amounts. But the certainty of this dollar income makes it uncertain in terms of real income, for the value and purchasing power of a dollar have, in recent years, continued to sink. A new form, the variable annuity, bases the annual payout on such a standard as the periodic valuation of securities set aside to fund the payments. Because of the uncertain track record of the securities markets in the past few years, variable annuities have not proved to be the inflation hedge some people had foreseen.

Federal income-tax treatment

For federal income-tax purposes, amounts received under an annuity are includable in gross income, except for the proportionate part of each amount that is considered to be a return of capital. The mathematical computation is based on the ratio that the amount invested in the annuity contract bears to its expected return at the time the annuity is deemed to start. For each contract there is a fixed exclusion ratio that continues until the death of the annuitant, or until the death of the last annuitant if the contract provides for payments to a survivor.

Take the example of an individual who has paid $12,650 for an annuity contract that provides for payments of $100 a month. Assuming that the expected return under contract is $16,000, his exclusion ratio is $\frac{\$12,650}{\$16,000}$, or 79.1 percent (79.06 rounded to the nearest tenth). If he receives 12 such monthly payments during the taxable year, the total amount excludable from his gross income that year is $949.20 ($1,200 times 79.1 percent). The balance of $250.80 ($1,200 minus $949.20) is included in his gross income. If he received only five payments of $100 during the year, he should exclude $395.50 ($500 times 79.1 percent) of the total received.

Federal estate-tax treatment

For federal estate-tax purposes, nothing is included in a decedent's gross estate if the annuity payments cease at his/her death, if there was no minimum number of payments guaranteed in the contract, leaving some payments still due at the time of death, and if this was a single-life annuity rather than a joint annuity where payments continue to a survivor. If the decedent had a survivorship annuity, the value of any amounts to be received by the survivor would be taxed to the decedent's estate, despite the fact that he himself had no further amounts to be paid to him under the contract. The value of the survivor's interest is, once more, based on life-expectancy tables.

Federal gift-tax treatment

An individual purchasing a commercial annuity that provides for survivorship payments to a designated party other than a spouse is deemed to have made a taxable gift to him/her of the value of the right to this income. Gifts, including annuity gifts, between spouses are completely gift-tax-free. In the case of a qualified employee benefit plan, however, the gift tax is not imposed.

Sale of your annuity

Although an annuity is a contract, its sale by the purchaser shortly before it matures (the point when annual or other stipulated payments by an insurance company will start) is deemed to produce ordinary income. If the purchaser sells his annuity contract at a loss (perhaps because he now has other sources of income and doesn't need it), no federal income tax deduction is allowed unless there is proof that his original purchase of the contract was a transaction entered upon for profit.

Employee annuities

One of the lesser-known provisions of the Pension Reform Act of 1974 deals with annuities. In the case of corporations subject to the act because they are doing business in interstate commerce, or have elected to be covered as a competitive measure, survivorship annuities must be offered to an employee who has been married for a year or more on the annuity starting date. The survivor annuity must not be less than one-half of the amount paid to the employee during the joint lives of himself and his spouse. This notification in the case of an employee who leaves his employment before reaching age 35 must be within "a reasonable period" after he leaves if distributions are made after December 31, 1989, although other times are specified for other distributions.

Periodic payouts will be less under a joint annuity than under a single-life annuity, so that the employee might elect not to have his spouse enjoy annuity coverage. In this case, the employer must inform him of the consequences of this election, using figures applicable to the individual employee.

However, if an employee is within 10 years of normal retirement age, he need not be offered the option of electing a single-life annuity rather than a survivorship annuity. In addition, a corporation's plan may provide that a joint and survivor annuity is the only form of benefit payable if an employee has been married for at least a year.

Private annuities

Some individuals are disinclined to purchase a commercial annuity—such as those discussed above—on the grounds that if the annuitant dies before his life expectancy, some or (in extreme cases) all of the payments that had been made to the insurance company or other provider will be thrown away—in the sense that the beneficiaries will get nothing of what he had paid out. A purchase of an annuity with a specified minimum number of payments guaranteed to be paid by the seller even if the annuitant himself should die is one way of assuring that the total cost of the annuity won't be at the expense of the beneficiaries. But the periodic return under an annuity of a specified cost will be less if a certain number of payments is guaranteed than if the contract is for one life, all payments to cease at the annuitant's death.

To keep all of his/her wealth in the family or available to beneficiaries, an individual may purchase a private annuity. This is sold by any party who is not engaged in the regular sale of annuity contracts. Most frequently, a private annuity contract is obtained from a relative or a friend, or from several of them, who are the intended beneficiaries. Then what the purchaser pays for the annuity will not be lost to the beneficiaries if he/she dies earlier than the date that is indicated in the life-expectancy table.

Substantial differences between commercial and private annuities should be noted: The operations and finances of an insurance company are closely regulated by state law. Certain reserves must be set up; investments are restricted; there are audits. Periodic payouts are based on generally accepted actuarial principles. There is every reason to believe that the annuitant will receive precisely what the contract for a commercial annuity specifies.

In the case of a private annuity, the provider of the contract may prove to be financially unable to make the payments when required. He/she may be dishonest. Since a private annuity rarely represents an arm's-length transaction between disinterested parties, the real relationship between the annuitant's cost and what he/she will receive is vague.

Income-tax treatment of private annuities

Most private annuities are unsecured. As a result, when an individual transfers properties to the provider of the contract, it is generally held that the former has no gain for federal income-tax purposes until he has recovered the cost of his annuity in the form of periodic payments. The annuitant is taxed when the amounts received exceed the cost of the property. If it is established that what the individual will receive is less than what the property transferred originally cost, he/she may be deemed to have made a taxable gift to the provider of the contract.

But under certain circumstances, a private annuity will represent the necessary certainty for characterization as an annuity. For example, the property transferred to the provider of the annuity payments may be prime real estate or investments that produce a regular return at least as high as the periodic payouts will be, and there is a restriction that the property cannot be sold or exchanged without the annuitant's permission. Here the value of what the annuitant will receive is determinable, and consequently he/she will have taxable gain if this figure is more than the purchase price of the property.

Conclusions and advice

• Consider purchasing a commercial annuity to provide yourself with income for life without fearing that your capital will be dissipated in later years. This device may protect your capital from creditors.

• If a relative or friend from whom you had "expectations" of inheriting property offers to give it to you at this time in return for providing him a certain amount periodically for as long as he lives, consider the proposition carefully. If you don't agree, he could subsequently lose the property. Or, instead of leaving it to you, he might give it to someone else who is agreeable to providing the annuity.

• Do not buy an annuity that will give you the income deemed necessary to live on without taking into account the fact that you may not have enough income after you've disposed of this capital, because of inflation or rising medical costs as you get older. A really good major-medical insurance policy could take care of the second of these problems.

• Do not transfer your property for a private annuity if you can't count on actually getting what had been promised to you. Honesty and good intentions on the part of the provider of the contract are not enough. He/she simply may not be in a position to deliver.

• Consider the present-day strength of the company from which you are considering the purchase of an annuity. Nonperforming real estate or dubious junk bonds held by an insurance company are matters that must be monitored these days.

• In a 1993 decision, actuarial tables were not used where the attending doctors estimated that when a taxpayer entered into the annuity arrangement, the chances that his cancer could be cured were not better than 2% or 3%. It was believed that he was not likely to survive more than one year.

Chapter Thirty-three

CHARITABLE REMAINDER WITH RIGHT OF INVASION

Prior to the Revenue Act of 1969, a useful tool of estate planning had been the charitable remainder with right of invasion. Typically, a husband could set up a trust for the life benefit of his spouse. Upon her death, the trust would terminate and the principal would go to one or more designated charitable organizations approved by the Internal Revenue Service. But the grantor was concerned about various contingencies that might make the provision he had made for the life tenant inadequate. Accordingly, the trust agreement empowered the trustee(s) to use as much of the principal as was necessary under defined and readily ascertainable external standards to meet the income beneficiary's extraordinary medical expenses or to maintain her existing standard of living in the face of inflation or the failure of her investments.

If the trust were created by the husband's will upon his death, a charitable-bequest deduction was allowed for the value of the property transferred to the trust, reduced by the value of the wife's life interest determined by the use of actuarial tables (taking into account the income that would go to the wife, discounted according to the remaining number of years in her life expectancy). Provided she had good major-medical insurance and her income from other sources together with her capital was sufficiently substantial to preclude the likelihood that she would need any of the trust principal, the probability that the charity would receive less than the full amount of the principal transferred to the trust was remote.

As a result, the decedent received a charitable-bequest deduction in accordance with the actuarial tables mentioned above. In short, this procedure took care of the annual income the decedent wished to provide, ultimate payouts of principal to charities selected by him, and a contingency plan to rechannel some, or even all, of the principal if additional income should ever be needed by the income beneficiary for reasons spelled out in the trust instrument.

A similar arrangement could also have been made while the grantor was still alive through the medium of an inter vivos trust. Under the circumstances just mentioned, his transfer to an approved charitable organization subject to his wife's life interest could provide a charitable deduction.

Such arrangements were called charitable remainders with right of invasion, because an approved charitable organization was the remainderman of a trust where the trustee could utilize principal under predetermined conditions not subject to the trustee's discretion to make further provision for the life tenant.

But the tax advantage of setting up a charitable remainder with right of invasion by the trustee no longer exists. Deduction is now allowed where there is a noncharitable income beneficiary, such as one's spouse, only if the trust is either a charitable-remainder annuity trust or a charitable remainder trust. (See Chapter Seven, "Charitable Remainder Trusts.") No provision can be made in the trust agreement for payments to individuals of amounts other than the stated annuity or fixed percentage amount.

Now let's consider this once-advantageous tax-deduction technique afresh. Yes, the former tax benefit is gone. The grantor's estate will no longer get any tax advantage from this procedure, nor will a charitable deduction be available in the case of the transfer to an inter vivos trust. But as an estate-planning tool, the charitable remainder trust still has a definite attractiveness.

Charitable remainder with invasion power still useful

An individual wants to provide someone, such as his spouse, with a certain amount of income for life. He doesn't want her to get the principal for any one or more of a number of possible reasons: She is not experienced in investment or property management or doesn't want to be bothered. She may be vulnerable to efforts by allegedly poor relations or by fortune hunters to get sizable chunks of her wealth. He does not want her to decide who is going to get the trust principal after her death, for he has very definite ideas of where any remaining money should go. He wants to leave that money to his church, or to a certain hospital or research foundation in which he is interested, or to his college.

But as much as he desires to leave wealth to his church or college, he wants even more to ensure that his wife's life income will not be short-changed by rampant inflation. He doesn't want her total income to be reduced because some of her investments turn out badly. And despite her own financial resources and her income from other sources, a catastrophic illness could wipe out the wife's financial means.

The mechanics

He sets up a charitable remainder trust with right of invasion, just as he would have done at the time when this device would have resulted in a tax benefit. What he is doing is providing for his wife in the amount he deems appropriate, with the principal being managed by experienced individuals, with no vulnerability to creditors' claims because the principal isn't either his or his wife's. After her death, the principal will go to his favorite charities, though without a tax deduction for his estate or himself. If the executor so elects, and the wife's income interest is a qualifying terminable interest, there could be a marital deduction. The trustee's power to invade for the surviving spouse's benefit would not cause loss of the marital deduction, even though she had no power of appointment over the principal. He may decide that even more than he wants to obtain a tax benefit, he wants the peace of mind (for himself and for his wife as income beneficiary) that comes with knowing that the real income he is providing for her can be maintained in the face of factors that might cause her to need more income as she gets older. He still hopes to provide for his favorite religious, charitable, or educational organizations, but his first priority is provision for his wife as income beneficiary. The tax benefit is deliberately forfeited to achieve this priority.

Use of a charitable-remainder annuity trust or unitrust can preserve the income-tax deduction. This should be worked out with your tax counsel.

Conclusions and advice

- Do not adopt the view that if a procedure was once attractive because of its tax benefit, that procedure loses all attractiveness once the benefit is no longer available.

- Consider, in the light of today's economy (and tomorrow's, insofar as this is possible), whether it is advisable for you to have a contingency plan in the event an income beneficiary's income proves to be insufficient.

- Consider your plan on a priorities basis. Which are you more interested in protecting, the income beneficiary or the charitable organization?

- Do not have a right of invasion power that is worded vaguely. This could lead to unpleasantness between the income beneficiary and the charitable remainderman.

- Property subject to a power of appointment is includible in gross estate if, at the time of his death, the holder could benefit himself, his estate, or the creditors of either, unless the power is limited by an ascertainable standard. Invasion of principal was permissible for the *continued* comfort, support, maintenance, or education of the beneficiary. By reason of the italicized word, he could not increase significantly his standard of living beyond what he had enjoyed before.

Chapter Thirty-four

CHARITABLE DEDUCTIONS THAT BENEFIT THE FAMILY

Bequests to individuals, such as members of the family or friends, are includable in a decedent's gross estate when he/she dies, while bequests to approved charitable organizations are a deduction, as is well known. Not so well known, however, is the fact that it is possible to get a federal estate-tax deduction for amounts that will be used for the benefit of the decedent's own relatives. Similarly, gifts to a trust can be tax-free if the purpose of the trust is charitable, such as making provisions for needy individuals.

A charitable bequest or contribution will not be lost merely because the decedent or donor stated a preference that first consideration in the allocation of trust funds for payouts be made to his/her own relations, if these relations otherwise qualify as the objects of legitimate charitable aid.

Charity can begin at home

The trust, testamentary or inter vivos, must be set up exclusively for a charitable purpose, such as providing educational assistance to students who are not financially able to go to college. The trustee(s) named by the grantor should be completely independent persons, or a trust company, and the trust should be irrevocable, with no reversionary or other powers retained by the grantor, so that it can be established that he/she has relinquished all control over the trust principal. Selection of the needy recipients of trust money is to be within the sole discretion of the trustee, but general guidelines can be set up, customarily in the trust agreement itself. Example: Recipients must be persons who are qualified for admission to college, trade school, or graduate school but lack the financial means to attend. Alternatively, there could be a condition that the total income of an applicant and his/her parents cannot exceed a specified amount.

Language used in court decisions

The grantor of a trust for charitable purposes is under no obligation to exclude from the benefits of the trust any relatives who may be in need of assistance. A court approved a charitable deduction where one trust agreement provided that the sole purpose was to fund university scholarships for high-school graduates "in need of help." The trustee was instructed to give preference to applicants having the same surname as the grantor, and who were related to him, but scholarships could be awarded to other qualified persons if no applicant meeting these qualifications made a claim. Although the testator plainly expressed a preference that properly qualified persons with his surname should have the first opportunity to benefit from the scholarships, his charity was not confined to such persons.

In another case, a woman's will declared: "I would like to set aside my Bank Stock as an educational loan fund...the dividend to be used to provide scholarship(s) first to relatives or other boys or girls...." This, ruled the court, merely indicated that a preference should be given to her relations, her charity not being confined to them. The need being met by the scholarships was the same for family and outside parties.

One decedent bequeathed the residue of her estate after specific bequests to a trustee, to pay the annual income therefrom to persons in need of financial assistance. The will then declared: "It is my wish that in carrying out the objects in the trust fund, preference be given to my relatives and friends who are in need of such aid and assistance." Deduction was allowed for a charitable bequest.

Language that forfeited the tax deduction

There is one very deep trap in this arrangement, however. In the situations just discussed, the only students eligible for assistance from the trust were those persons who lacked the means to attend college. If money can be channeled by the trust to relatives or friends who are not in financial need, then the trust is not being used exclusively for charitable purposes. Deduction, therefore, is denied.

The charitable-bequest deduction was denied in the case of one trust that was set up "for the education of my grandchildren and for the education of deserving boys and girls.... However, if at any time the net income from this trust is in excess of the amount required to provide college educations for those of my grandchildren who then desire same...I desire that my Trustee shall use the balance of said net income to provide...scholar-ships...to worthy boys and girls...who without financial assistance would be unable to attend college." Here there was no requirement of a showing for need for family members, but there was for other applicants. This discrimination was what led to the denial of the deduction.

No deduction was allowed for a transfer to a tax-exempt trust, where the grantor stated that it was his wish "to make provision to assist in the college education of his grandnieces and grandnephews...." There were 12 children actually enrolled in and attending a college. Any amounts not expended for these persons would be available for admittedly proper purposes of the trust. But the grantor had written that he "contemplates that the payments herein directed will substantially exhaust both principal and income of the trust hereby created." The trust was deemed to have been used primarily for noncharitable purposes, and as a result the charitable deduction was lost.

A similar finding was made where a trust was set up, the funds being used in the first instance to pay for the college education of designated relatives. After their education had been completed and financed, the remainder in the trust fund was to go to a named college to be used for scholarships, preference to be given to relatives of the grantor.

Trust for benefit of employees first

An alternative to setting up a trust for the benefit of needy individuals, with preference to be given to family members, is a trust for the benefit of the children of one's employees. This might also cover children of employees of a corporation in which the grantor is a substantial stockholder. One decedent's will set up a trust to provide scholarships for students who desired education in vocational or agricultural studies. The trustees were to award scholarships to students who were the decedent's employees or their descendants, a requirement that was to be waived in favor of any other students only if insufficient employees made application. The bequest qualified for deduction, being for the benefit of a general class as distinguished from mere benevolence to employees, as long as the general class to be benefited (nonemployees) was not so small that the community didn't benefit from the aid given to students.

Conclusions and advice

- Make certain that the trust instrument restricts beneficiaries to those who are in need. Family members must be subject to the same conditions, although they can be given top priority among candidates.

- Establish guidelines similar to those that would be used in any objective selection of eligible individuals.

- Do not indicate in the trust agreement or elsewhere that the real purpose of the transfer is to benefit family or friends, or that it is not anticipated that there will be funds available for outsiders. This may be the grantor's opinion, but it should not appear as part of the stated arrangement.

Chapter Thirty-five

AVOIDING DISALLOWANCE OF CHARITABLE BEQUESTS

Charitable bequests can be an important part of one's estate planning from several points of view. These bequests can reduce gross estate while implementing a benevolent purpose of the decedent. Lifetime charitable contributions reduce the donor's income and similarly serve his/her benevolent desires. But bequests offer greater opportunities, for there is no percentage limitation on the amount of the deduction for federal estate-tax purposes as there is in the case of the income tax. This chapter describes how the various benefits available through charitable bequests can be saved from forfeiture through careful planning.

Definition of a charitable organization

Deduction is allowed from gross estate for transfers to or for the use of any organization operated exclusively for religious, charitable, scientific, literary, or educational purposes, if no part of its earnings is used for the benefit of any individual and no substantial part of its activities involves the carrying on of propaganda or other attempts to influence legislation. The donor or his/her adviser must check on the true nature of the organization and what it does with its money to ensure that the deduction will be allowed by the Internal Revenue Service.

In the case of contributions after December 31, 1986, of certain interests in real property to charitable organizations, to the United States, or to a state or local government unit, deduction is allowed for federal estate- and gift-tax purposes even if the contributions do not meet the requirement for deductibility for federal income-tax purposes that the contribution be used for conservation purposes.

A charitable bequest is limited to an organization or to a political subdivision of the United States. But a gift in trust may be made for a foreign political unit when this gift is restricted to charitable purposes. Example: A US resident makes a bequest to a trust for the benefit of a home for the aged in a certain community in Germany.

Exclusively for charitable purposes

That a particular organization is being operated exclusively for charitable or similar purposes cannot be assumed from the name or general activities of the organization. For example, a county medical society may perform charitable work for the community while performing personal services for physicians that are hardly of a charitable nature: serving as a collection agency, giving seminars on running an office and other economic matters, publishing advice on doctors' tax questions, and the like. Similarly, a state bar association may provide legal services for the needy, but lobbying for legislation favorable to lawyers is also carried on, referral and telephone answering services are furnished, and a group insurance program for member attorneys is sponsored. These organizations, despite their public services, are not being operated exclusively for charitable purposes.

It's not charitable if you get something in return

There is no deduction for a charitable bequest or contribution when the charitable donor gets something in return. The deduction will be disallowed if the donor has reserved the right to receive something, as in a case where money was given to a certain hospital "for the establishment of free room or rooms, first, for the persons named as beneficiaries of this trust, and then, for such other persons as the Board of Directors of said hospital may from time to time direct." This was not just a preference for needy relatives or friends; it took care of them whether or not they were in need. (See Chapter Thirty-four, "Charitable Deductions That Benefit the Family.")

The result is the same where the donor had neither asked nor expected to receive anything in return. If a grateful hospital administrator notifies the executor that facilities will always be available without charge to members of the donor's family, the executor should write an immediate reply that nothing was expected or will be accepted.

Estate or donor must trigger the deduction

To be deductible, the money or other property must pass from the estate or donor to a charitable organization because of action by the party seeking the deduction. The benevolence must have been his. In one case, a decedent's will directed his executor to erect a monument for him in Israel, and the executor decided instead to establish an endowed scholarship fund for Jewish students. Deduction for money going for a permissible purpose was denied because the decedent was not the one who decided to transfer funds for a charitable purpose. Language in a will, trust instrument, or letter saying that the decedent knew his spouse and children would make gifts in his name to his favorite charities, for which reason he left the entire estate to the family, did not create deductions for the estate when the decedent's wishes were implemented by the family just as he had expected them to be. The deduction was also lost where a will directed the executor, a lifelong friend of the decedent, to take care of certain charitable organizations in which it was known that the decedent had been interested.

Charitable deduction is what charity actually gets

Sometimes a decedent's will provides for bequests to a charitable organization. But a relative may challenge the provision, saying that undue influence had been exercised on the decedent by a hospital or church when his/her powers of resistance were low. To avoid unpleasant publicity, the charitable organization may agree to accept a smaller amount than called for by the will, the balance going to the family. The charitable deduction is limited to what is received by the charity. To prevent this situation, an individual may provide in his/her will that if any beneficiary seeks to challenge the validity of the will, the amount designated for him/her will go instead to someone else, such as the remainderman.

Bequest must be unconditional

No deduction is allowed for a charitable bequest that is conditional if there is a real possibility that the condition will not be met. One individual left her home to an approved organization, subject to its agreement that the home would be maintained in its existing condition. In the absence of such assurance, the bequest wasn't deductible. Nor was deduction allowed for a bequest to a church of a certain denomination in a named community, where there was no such church at the time of the bequest nor any certainty that there ever would be.

Discrimination

In recent years there has been a great increase in the disallowance of charitable bequests on the ground that the recipient organization was practicing some form of discrimination. That would mean, in effect, that the organization was not being operated exclusively for charitable purposes. Example: a charitable, religious, or educational organization that does not admit or accept persons who are not white.

The Internal Revenue Service sells on a subscription basis Publication No. 78, listing organizations to which deductible contributions are allowed. But this list is constantly being revised, and many organizations once listed have had their names removed because of discrimination of some sort. At a time when an individual plans his/her estate, reference to this list may show that certain organizations are approved. Bequests are provided in the will in reliance upon this. But by the time the decedent dies, and the bequests are implemented, the organization may no longer be recognized as acceptable. It is the responsibility of an individual or his/her adviser to periodically check the status of organizations to which bequests are to be made. If the individual wants to have the bequest allowed as a tax deduction, he/she should replace the names of stricken organizations with other charitable organizations in good standing. An individual whose interest in a particular organization is sufficiently great to permit him to ask questions, or whose potential bequests would indicate that he has the right to request answers, should obtain an affirmative statement from an organization that it is not practicing discrimination. Some organizations do not wait to be asked but inform the public of their eligibility to receive a deductible bequest or contribution through mailings or advertisements.

The importance of making certain that bequests are not made to institutions practicing discrimination is highlighted by the fact that anyone who knows of such a situation can trigger the disallowance. The US Supreme Court has held that any interested party can bring suit to enjoin the Secretary of the Treasury from approving or continuing on its list of eligible organizations any organization that engages in discriminatory practices. A private school, for example, may be called upon to state specifically that it doesn't engage in any kind of discrimination. That can no longer be assumed. The issue as to whether the US Treasury may properly deny charitable status to a religious school that practices discrimination as part of its religious belief was pending in the Supreme Court in the fall of 1982.

State law may restrict charitable bequests

Under the laws of some states, an individual with a spouse, descendant, or parent cannot bequeath more than one-half of his/her estate to charity, a bequest for a larger amount being valid only up to the 50 percent mark. Elsewhere, bequests for religious or charitable purposes made by will less than 30 days prior to a decedent's death are void, the property then going to the residuary legatee or next of kin.

Conclusions and advice

• Check, and keep checking, the actual practices of organizations to which significant bequests are to be made. If the amount of the deduction is worth getting, so is the time spent in verifying entitlement.

• Name an alternative beneficiary if the original one may not be given the funds designated. One individual's will left property to a state college (an approved organization) to provide an annual scholarship for a white Caucasian with the same surname as the decedent. If no such person applied for the scholarship in a particular year, the funds were to be used for an athletic scholarship. The deduction was allowed. The trustee could not perform its fiduciary duties by selecting someone with the decedent's original specifications without violating its higher authority as an agency of the state not to practice discrimination. The money, therefore, could not be used for a racially discriminatory purpose but had to go instead to a deserving athlete.

• Ascertain whether a conditional bequest will be accepted by the named beneficiary. If not, make other dispositions.

• Where property that can't readily be marketed is given to a charitable organization, advise the organization of where and how it can best be sold if necessary. The amount of the deduction depends on the fair market value of the asset. If the charitable organization wants to convert the asset into cash quickly, sale may be made at a woefully inadequate price because of lack of knowledge of how it should be made. The full amount of the deduction may be protected if the donee is told of the best available market for, say, a collection of Egyptian scarabs from the Fourth Dynasty.

• Make certain that the bequest goes from the decedent or his/her estate to the charity. Example: A father left property to his son, who was a member of a religious order that takes an oath of poverty. The son turned the property over to his order, which was an approved charitable organization. There was no allowable deduction, but there would have been had the father left the property directly to the order instead of to his son.

• Do not be led by the name of an organization, or the excellence of its public works, to believe that it qualifies as a charitable organization for the purpose of a deduction.

• Do not permit anything to be received, or even offered, in return for a charitable bequest or contribution. If the donee organization unilaterally offers services or anything else in return, they should be declined at once.

• In order that the charitable deduction be recognized, an individual should be familiar with the consequences of undervaluation of property.

• The donee of contributed property is now required to report the receipt of noncash property and how much was subsequently received when the property was sold. This can compromise the amount of the contribution claimed by the donor.

• A 1994 case held that in the case of jewelry owned by the decedent, the value to be used is the price at which the items, or comparable ones, would be sold at retail.

Chapter Thirty-six

POWERS OF APPOINTMENT

One of the most sought-after ideals of estate planning is to have your wishes carried out according to your desires after you are no longer here, in the light of facts and figures that may not be known to you at the time of your death. One way of attempting to accomplish this is to empower another person to act at a later date or dates in accordance with what you would have done under the circumstances had you been alive (or mentally competent). This other person must be familiar with your objectives, aspirations, and prejudices, and he/she must be in a position to see that they are carried out as far as money or other property have been made available for the purpose. Additionally or alternatively, you can set up specific guidelines or requests at this time for this person to follow, using as much discretion as you may choose to confer upon him/her to make judgments in the light of changing circumstances.

A deputy to act as you would have done

For example, you don't know right now which of your children or other relatives or friends you'd most like to help in view of their plans, financial situation, and character. Do you really want all of your children or grandchildren to share your wealth equally when their needs, capabilities, and pattern of life may be quite different? Will you be able to channel your property primarily or entirely to a beneficiary who fulfills your wish by going into the family business or entering medical school?

Nature of a power of appointment

You may give someone the authority to say who will get the property that you place under his/her right of disposition. This is called a power of appointment, although it need not be so labeled. For example, by will or by deed of trust, you create a trust and give someone (called the holder of the power of appointment) the right to say who will get the property or its income, in what amounts, and at what times. If the holder is restricted in his selections to designated parties or classes of persons (such as blood relatives of the grantor), he holds a special power of appointment. If he can name himself, his estate, or the creditors of either, he holds a general power of appointment. Where he is authorized to give ("appoint") the property to anyone he believes the creator of the power might have selected if he still were here to make a choice, that is a general power of appointment, for "anyone" could include the holder of the power.

Bestowal of a power of appointment upon a relative, a close friend, or a business associate gives the grantor great flexibility in his/her estate planning. He has not committed himself to the future distribution of designated property or income to those who might not need it at the time the distribution is made, or who might not use their new wealth wisely.

After the creator of the power has died, the property he/she designated for apportionment can be held in trust until the holder of the power sees fit to exercise it. For example, the creator may authorize his/her brother to distribute the designated property at the time the youngest of the creator's children reaches age 21. One of the children may have married a very wealthy person and has no financial needs. One lives a simple, isolated life and has no monetary yearnings. One has developed what appears to be a permanent physical disability. One may have manifested great artistic talent that years of costly study would probably bring to fruition. The choice of parties to whom property can be given (appointed) may be spelled out to include any related person. One of these may have joined a religious or political group to which the decedent had been violently opposed. Another offended the decedent's ideals about lifestyle or patriotism. These are merely a few instances. The holder of the power should be someone who knows what the decedent would have done about distributing his/her property had he/she been in a position to know all of the facts and circumstances at the time.

Advantages of power of appointment

The creator of the power, obviously, may benefit greatly from it. In addition to flexibility, he/she can avoid having to make hard decisions, such as cutting out of his will a son who had been offensive. Let the holder of the power make the decision to bypass that son. By using a power of appointment, the creator may have his property apportioned without his own personal biases, which he realizes could result in inequities or injustice.

Disadvantages of power of appointment

But there can be disadvantages in granting a power of appointment. The property may actually be distributed without regard to the decedent's wishes. If the holder were empowered to give the assets to anyone if the creator's children didn't seem to be living up to the decedent's standards, he might bestow the property on his own daughter. If it is a general power of appointment, the holder could act selfishly and appoint himself. Finally, the principle may fail to work: The property might pass in a way that would have disappointed the deceased.

Danger of accepting a general power of appointment

Advantageous as a power of appointment may be to the creator, it may place a substantial tax burden on the holder's estate. There is no risk in accepting a special power of appointment. But if an individual has a general power of appointment at the time of his death, any property that is subject to his discretionary distribution will be includable in his own gross estate, for it represents property that could have gone to him up to the moment of his death and was still under his control at that time. The same is true in the case of property that he had appointed to other persons within three years of his death, even though the general rule of inclusion of gifts within three years of death is no longer in effect.

Why should someone accept a general power of appointment in view of this great tax risk? Usually it is because he doesn't understand the gravity of the estate-tax risk. For example, his authority may be to distribute property to the decedent's children in such amounts, if any, that they may require or, alternatively, to anyone else whose views and moral conduct would not have been obnoxious to the decedent. The holder of the power hadn't been authorized in so many words to give property to himself, so even if he had some modest knowledge of powers of appointment, he might not have recognized his authority as being a general power. But it is, because "anyone" includes himself.

Or someone may accept designation as holder of a general power because he/she believes that he/she will distribute all of the property for the benefit of others before he/she dies. He/she may be right, but there's no assurance that he/she will live for three years after the power becomes effective. Or he/she may not realize that he/she can refuse to accept a general power created without his/her knowledge in the decedent's will, or how and when to do this. Or he/she may feel such a sense of responsibility to the decedent or to his/her family that he/she accepts the power despite its risks.

Exercise of power of appointment

Exercising a general power of appointment so that the property subject to it won't be in the holder's gross estate when he/she dies may be difficult or even impossible. The holder's authorization may have been to distribute the property at such time as the decedent's youngest child has reached majority under the laws of the state where he/she lives. At the time the decedent dies and the holder of the power has property under his/her discretionary powers, one child is three years old. The holder can't act to free his/her estate from tax risk for many years: He/she could die before the child outgrows his/her minority.

In addition, the holder of the power might expect to exercise it in favor of others at the end of the year, when she can evaluate the decedent's business according to its earnings or net worth at that time. Or he/she might wish to wait for a few years so that he/she can form an opinion as to the capabilities of various relatives of the decedent. But before this takes place, the holder becomes mentally incompetent and can't exercise the power. The property is still subject to his/her disposition when he/she dies 15 years later, even though in all that period the holder may have lacked the legal competence to act.

Where a trust instrument provides that the income beneficiary may have free access to the trust's principal, the holder has a general power of appointment because he/she has the power to appoint to him/herself property that would otherwise go to different people. A power to withdraw principal that is limited to an ascertainable standard relating to health, education, support, or maintenance is not a general power. In determining whether a power is limited by an ascertainable standard, it is immaterial whether the beneficiary is required to exhaust his/her other income before the power can be exercised.

Renunciation

An individual can renounce his designation as the holder of a general power of appointment as soon as he learns that he has been designated, although because of a sense of obligation to a relative or friend, he may not choose to do so. (See Chapter Thirty-seven, "Disclaimers and Renunciations.") Or he may petition a state court to change the general power to a special one; but there is no assurance that the court will do so, or that it will act quickly enough to prevent estate-tax liability.

How the Internal Revenue Service knows

An individual may accept a general power of appointment in the belief that the Internal Revenue Service will never know that he has it. But one of the questions the executor must answer on the federal estate-tax return is, "Did the decedent ever possess, exercise, or release any general power of appointment?" Now the cat is out of the bag. The fact that an individual holds a general power of appointment may not be known to him, or he may long since have forgotten it. This is one of the many reasons an individual should review the questions to be answered when his own estate-tax return is filed. (See Chapter Forty-three, "The Dry Run.")

Conclusions and advice

• If you have it in mind to create a power of appointment, sound out your candidates for holders of the power to ensure that they will accept. If they are doubtful, designate others who are agreeable.

• If you are asked whether you will accept a power of appointment, or told that you have been given one, consult an attorney who is knowledgeable in this area.

• In the event you are named as the holder of a general power, make a prompt disclaimer if you are unwilling to assume the tax risks.

• Do not accept a general power of appointment. When you are asked, say emphatically that you will be pleased to offer your services, but only if it is a special power.

• Do not assume that you will be able to avoid estate-tax liability by prompt exercise of a general power in someone else's favor.

Chapter Thirty-seven

DISCLAIMERS AND RENUNCIATIONS

Disclaimers figure in many aspects of estate planning. If a decedent properly disclaimed an interest in property, its value is not included in his gross estate. An individual can't dispose of his property according to his own desires if a beneficiary subsequently disclaims what has been provided for him, unless a successor beneficiary was named by the transferor in order to take this possibility into account. The marital deduction may be affected by disclaimers of either the surviving spouse or third parties. Disclaimers can be important in the case of gifts and powers of appointment.

In view of the many tax aspects of disclaimers, it seems strange that prior to 1977 there were no definitive rules as to what constitutes a disclaimer; nor were there rules of general application concerning the tax consequences of a disclaimer. The disclaimer rules now cover the federal estate tax, the gift tax, and the generation-skipping tax.

What is a disclaimer?

A disclaimer is a complete, unqualified refusal to accept rights to which one is entitled. It is a disavowal, denial, or renunciation of an interest, right, or property imputed to an individual or alleged to be his/hers.

Gross estate

Gross estate includes the value of all of a decedent's property, wherever located, to the extent of his/her interest at the time of death. If a lifetime or after-death transfer is valid, a disclaimer of property receivable by gift or inheritance is not treated as a taxable transfer by the person making the disclaimer.

If a decedent inherited property from someone else, the value can be kept out of the former's gross estate even without his having renounced acceptance if his executor disclaims it within the permissible time, provided that state law authorizes the executor to take such action. In one case a husband left one-third of his property to his wife, and she died within three hours after he did as the result of a common disaster. Her executrix immediately renounced on behalf of the wife the interest passing from her husband, and that amount was not includable in the wife's gross estate.

The marital deduction

The marital deduction is based upon *what* passes from a decedent to a surviving spouse, not *why* this was so. If a decedent's surviving spouse makes a disclaimer of any property interest that would otherwise be considered as passing from the decedent to his spouse, the disclaimed interest is considered as having passed from the decedent to the person(s) entitled to receive the interest as the result of the disclaimer. One decedent's second wife agreed to give up her interest in her husband's estate for $40,000 in favor of his other heirs, and that is all she received. That was the extent allowable for the marital deduction for tax purposes, although the will had left her a considerably larger figure.

A decedent's widow renounced the provisions of his will and elected to exercise her dower rights. In connection with this renunciation, other beneficiaries agreed to pay her a specified amount each month for the remainder of her life. The mathematical value of these payments could not be taken on the husband's estate-tax return as the marital deduction, because the promise to pay them was not owed by her husband in his lifetime and was not a liability of his estate.

If an interest passes from the decedent to his surviving spouse as a result of a disclaimer by a third party, such as a son, the interest is considered as passing from the decedent to his surviving spouse, thus qualifying for the marital deduction. A reason for the disclaimer: The son might have decided that his mother was inadequately financed, while he could do without the money.

Charitable bequests

In order for an estate to be entitled to a charitable deduction, the money must flow from the estate to the charity by reason of the decedent's decision and act. As noted in Chapter Thirty-five, "Avoiding Disallowance of

Charitable Bequests," one father left a portion of his estate to his children in equal amounts. His son was a member of a religious order who had taken an oath of poverty, and he turned his inheritance over to the order. Presumably the father had anticipated that this would happen. But the father's estate wasn't entitled to the charitable deduction, because the money did not flow from him or his estate to the charity.

But the funds do go from the estate to the charity where the intervening party between them disclaims his interest so that, in default of the named beneficiary, the charity receives the bequest directly. A charitable deduction is allowed where a beneficiary disclaimed his bequest if the charity had already been named in the will as a secondary, successor, or contingent beneficiary. As a result, this renunciation simultaneously benefits the charity, reduces gross estate, and lowers the federal estate tax.

Estate planning should consider the possibility that a beneficiary will not want, and will refuse to accept, property left to him/her by will. Examples: stock in a nuclear-power-plant corporation or in a company that does business in a foreign country that practices racial discrimination. If the named successor or contingent beneficiaries also disclaim the bequest, possibly for the same reason, the unclaimed property will go to the state. The decedent has gained no advantage by this. He could have named a charitable organization as a contingent beneficiary. If the bequest then went to the charity after other renunciations, the estate would get a deduction for a charitable bequest.

Powers of appointment

Gross estate includes the value of any property "with respect to which the decedent has at the time of his death, a general power of appointment," according to the Internal Revenue Code. (See Chapter Thirty-six, "Powers of Appointment.") So if an individual was given a general power of appointment over someone else's property, he may have included in his own gross estate the value of property that he never in fact owned.

A disclaimer of a general power of appointment is not a taxable transfer. But the exercise of such a power to any extent by the holder of the power is treated as an acceptance of its benefits, so that a disclaimer can't subsequently be made. The acceptance of any consideration in return for making the disclaimer is treated as an acceptance of the benefits of the interest disclaimed.

The federal gift tax

A refusal to accept ownership of property that is offered does not constitute the making of a gift by the person making the refusal to the person who eventually gets the property. The intended donee did not have to accept the gift. But those entitled to receive property by action of certain state intestacy laws have no power to prevent themselves from becoming the owners, and hence they have made gifts when they "let" other persons receive the property. Example: A father's will left his property to his son. The will was invalid and the property, under the state intestacy law, went to the next of kin, who was also the son. The son disclaimed his right to the property, which went to the decedent's next closest kin, the decedent's grandson. The son was deemed to have made a taxable gift to his own son by renouncing in the latter's favor. Under the intestacy law, the property became the son's, and he couldn't refuse to be bound by the state law. So when he thought he was renouncing his interest, he was merely making a gift of it. The result of this case would probably be different under current law, which recognizes a disclaimer qualified under federal law, even though it fails as a disclaimer under state law.

In other examples, an individual who had made no will proposed to leave practically his entire estate to his son to equalize to some extent the financial worth of his survivors. The family agreed to the proposal, and an attorney prepared a will. Before it was signed by the father, however, he died. His wife and daughter, realizing that some affirmative action was necessary to carry out the decedent's wishes, renounced their interests in the estate, which would then go to them under state laws of intestacy in the absence of a valid will. The entire estate then went to the son. It was held that the widow and daughter each had made a gift to the son of their respective interests in the decedent's estate. They had been without power to disclaim an interest that, under their state's laws of intestacy, was theirs. (Not all states have such laws; check with an attorney to confirm your local law.)

When a husband and wife own property jointly with the right of survivorship, the survivor can't avoid gift tax by renouncing his/her interest after the death of the other spouse, so the property goes to the children as next of kin, if, as is generally the case, state law does not provide for their renunciation of rights previously accepted.

In both the above cases, current federal law would recognize the qualified disclaimers even though they did not satisfy state law.

More than intent is required to disclaim

Renunciation involves more than one's statement. A disclaimer was not recognized when a life beneficiary of a trust with a right of invasion of principal filed an affidavit stating that she had "no intention of invading the principal of the decedent's estate for any purpose whatsoever." This was not deemed to be a complete and absolute refusal to accept the right to make use of trust principal.

Requirements for a disclaimer

In order for a disclaimer to be recognized for federal tax purposes, these ground rules must be met:

1. The refusal must be in writing.

2. The written disclaimer must be received by the transferor of the interest (such as the executor of the decedent's estate) or the holder of the legal title to the property not later than nine months after the date on which the transfer creating the interest is made. This period extends to nine months after the day on which the person making the disclaimer has reached age 21, if he/she was a minor when the transfer took place. A transfer is considered to be made when it is treated as a completed gift for federal gift-tax purposes, or upon the date of the decedent's death in the case of a bequest.

3. The person must not have accepted the interest or any of its benefits before making the disclaimer.

4. The interest must pass to someone other than the person making the disclaimer as a result of the refusal to accept the property. For purposes of this requirement, the person making the disclaimer can't have

the authority to direct the redistribution or transfer of the property to another person and be treated as making a "qualified" disclaimer. Under a 1978 change in the law, a widow refused to accept all or a portion of her interest in property passing from her late husband and, as a result of this refusal, the property passed to a trust in which she had an income interest. Her disclaimer kept the value of this property out of her gross estate.

Disclaimer can protect property from IRS seizure

Where one individual disclaimed an inheritance, which thereupon went (under state law) to his son, the next of kin, a significant tax benefit was obtained. The father owed back federal taxes, and the Internal Revenue Service sought to impose a tax lien on the property he had inherited. But because of the disclaimer, it was never his property and the Service couldn't touch it. Without the disclaimer, the property would probably never have gone to the son.

Conclusions and advice

• Act quickly in disclaiming property or in getting legal advice as to what you should do.

• Make provisions for contingent beneficiaries in your will, so that your property will go to persons of your choice if the named beneficiaries disclaim their interests.

• Do not make use of any part of an interest before disclaiming it. Also, do not accept any consideration in return for making the disclaimer. This would be treated as an acceptance of the benefits of the interests disclaimed, and no disclaimer is possible after acceptance.

Chapter Thirty-eight

VALUATION OF ESTATE ASSETS

An individual, of course, wants to leave as large an estate as possible for his/her beneficiaries. But he should plan to minimize the tax erosion brought on by valuations that are higher than they need to be. He should take steps at this time to keep down those valuations upon which estate tax will be based.

The executor who will insert values on your federal estate-tax return is not likely to be as familiar as you are with the details of your assets. The same is probably true of his/her professional advisers. Now is the time to see that your specialized knowledge and experience are available to these people. Despite the professional competence of your executor or his/her advisers, you have the unique opportunity now of accentuating the negative to reduce your gross estate for tax purposes.

Documentation of the minus factors

Perhaps you have tried to dispose of certain of your properties. During the process of negotiations, defects or shortcomings may have been uncovered. Yet on the filing date of your estate-tax return, your executor may be unaware of these facts. Describe them now in a letter that you write to your executor-to-be. (See Chapter Forty-four, "A Letter to Your Executor.") Or you might prefer to record the same information in documents that will become part of your tax paperwork. Keep correspondence or other papers that explain why prospective purchasers wouldn't buy your property or for what reason they were unwilling to pay a figure approximating fair market value at the time.

Here are some examples:

• Real estate. Indicate reasons for a belief that title may be clouded, even though this is not disclosed in a title search. In certain sections of the country, there is serious question about the validity of title to lands transferred by Native Americans during the 18th century. There may be disputes or claims that have not yet ripened into litigation and that would not be known to outside parties, even the experts. There may be boundary squabbles with which you are familiar but an appraiser is not. Are you familiar with zoning peculiarities not generally known? For example, a property may be used for commercial purposes under a grandfather clause only if used for the existing function, but the property would be limited to residential use if the function should be changed. That would seriously affect the value of the property.

You may be familiar with efforts of aggressive environmentalist groups that could limit the use of property, even though this possibility is not yet generally realized. Because of your interest in this particular property, you could be aware of pending legislation that might adversely affect the attractiveness of the property, or you may have knowledge of forthcoming limitations on the availability of utility services.

Present access to the property may only be by a road through the lands of relatives and friends. If you disposed of the property, the new owner might be denied this access and hence would buy the land only at a price reflective of the need for heavy cash outlays for a new road.

Though low, rentals from your property may be frozen by a long-term lease, possibly with a renewal clause at the same figure at the tenant's option. This would make your property less valuable than similar land where there is a more realistic lease with more realistic rental terms.

Your property may be held in co-ownership with other parties who are notoriously difficult to work with. Your executor or his/her adviser is not likely to know this. But such a state of affairs could well discourage a potential purchaser except at a price discounted to reflect the unpleasant co-ownership fact.

Facilities may appear to be in average condition, but you are aware that costly repairs or replacements are essential. Let this be known to your executor-to-be.

If appropriate to your situation, compile a list of past owners of the property and the uniformly poor experience they have had with it. If the property has consistently proved to be a "loser" for previous owners, buyers will probably not be willing to tempt fate except at an irresistible bargain.

The property may have defects known only to you at this time.

• Special-use property. Real estate must be valued for federal estate-tax purposes according to its highest and best use. In consequence, your property may be valued according to what it would have been worth had you used it for a different purpose. Property may be valued for estate-tax purposes according to its present use, providing that certain specific conditions exist; the value of a farm or the real-estate assets of a closely-held business must meet stipulated guidelines if the property has been owned by a decedent or a member of his family (which may include a nephew) for five of the eight years prior to the decedent's death, disability, or the date he/she started to receive Social Security benefits, whichever is earliest. A surviving spouse's cash rental of specially-valued real property to a member of his/her family is not treated as a cessation of a qualified use.

The tax benefit of a lower valuation is available only if the property passes to a qualified heir, as defined in the tax law, and there are requirements as to what he/she does with the property. Establishment of prior ownership and use requires accumulation of data, and the percentage that the value of the property bears to the decedent's total assets must meet prescribed rules. This is a highly technical subject not appropriate for discussion here, except in general. Ask your tax adviser to work out with you the possibility of having real estate devoted to farming or closely-held business use valued according to present use. If necessary, ask him/her to research Sections 2032A and 6324B of the Internal Revenue Code. Understanding the possibility of obtaining a lower valuation under this procedure is something that can affect the amount of estate taxes that will ultimately have to be provided for. In order to qualify for the substantial-compliance rule, the election need only have been made on a federal estate-tax return that was filed on time.

• Listed stocks. Ordinarily, securities listed on a recognized exchange or traded actively on an over-the-counter market are valued for estate-tax purposes at the mean trading price on the date of death or on the alternate valuation date. In some cases, courts have held that a valuation lower than the New York Stock Exchange mean for a particular stock may be used because of factors known to insiders but still unknown to traders whose activities set the current price on the critical valuation date.

An individual may own such a large block of stock that it could not be sold within a reasonable time without depressing the market value. Under the rule of blockage, the IRS may have to accept a lower valuation of this block than the mean between highest and lowest prices of the stock on the valuation date. Such valuation could be established by a broker handling secondary distribution through an underwriter. He/she should be asked about the probable cost to the estate of such a distribution, and what percentage markdown in the value of the securities might be expected under the blockage rule. This blockage discount, if accepted by the IRS, will reduce the valuation of the stock for estate-tax purposes.

Sometimes an individual owns shares acquired at a price below market in return for an agreement that he/she will not sell the stock for a certain length of time. This stock may be valued at a discount for estate-tax purposes as restricted or investment-letter shares. Advise your executor if you have stock of this character. Generally the shares are imprinted with wording that refers to the restriction, but the executor may not actually see the certificates when filing the estate-tax return.

A corporation, the shares of which are listed on a recognized exchange, may have issued some stock that had never been registered with the Securities & Exchange Commission, for any number of reasons, perhaps only to eliminate the accounting, legal, and printing expenses of registering a new issue. Unregistered stock has limited marketability, so a discount is applied in arriving at a valuation for estate-tax purposes. Advise your executor if your shares happen to be unregistered, or he/she may value them at a figure that is too high.

• Stocks of closely-held corporations. If a corporation's stock is not listed on an active market, there is no ready way of arriving at a valuation. An individual who owns such stock must lay the foundation now for establishing that his/her shares need not be valued according to some standard formula such as net worth, capitalized earnings, or comparison with the value of an actively traded stock, because of certain factors that affect the shares in a negative way. Examples:

This corporation is a one-man company. Upon the owner's death, without a competent backup team, the stock would have limited appeal to investors. The company's product line lacks diversification. The physical plant is antiquated, requiring considerable investment. The indicated earnings are not a proper basis for calculating value because there has been large income of a nonrecurring nature. The company is heavily involved in lawsuits alleging product liability, patent infringement, and the like, and counsel is not encouraging about what the courts will decide. The books have never been audited by an independent certified accountant and hence couldn't be accepted by the investing public as reliable indicators of the company's true financial condition. There are pending tax assessments that could require the payout of substantial sums. The company has never paid a dividend, which is an unattractive feature for an investor seeking a source of income. Depreciation and other reserves are woefully inadequate. You may know of these value depressants, but your executor and his/her accountant could very well not know about all of them. Keep a memorandum where it can be made available to the executor at such time as it is needed to reduce estate-tax valuations.

Your executor may not know, as you do, that there is in effect a buy-sell agreement, under which the estate will have to sell your stock back to the corporation or to the surviving shareholders at a formula price that could be far less than the stock may be worth at the time of your death, or even retirement. (See Chapter Twenty-two, "Buy-Sell Agreements.") This is binding on your estate. The requirement may be contained in a corporate bylaw or in an old letter from the company to you, the existence of which the executor has no reason to suspect. On the plus side, the existence of such an agreement limits the estate-tax valuation to the figure in the buy-sell agreement. Let your executor know about it.

Sometimes a corporate bylaw or a stockholder agreement will provide that no shareholder can sell a stock without giving the corporation or other shareholders the right of first refusal at whatever price any outside party offers for the stock. Tell your executor. The existence of such a provision will limit what an investor might offer for the shares, for he/she would be disinclined to investigate a corporation fully at his own expense if his offer could be a waste of time and other parties would merely have to match it without exploratory costs.

Sometimes, though, stock in a corporation is purchased at a certain price in an arm's-length transaction. Such sales cannot be regarded as indicating a buyer's concept of true value; actually this person was bidding for something more than the shares themselves. Perhaps the buyer wanted to acquire enough stock so as to be able to control the corporation in order to provide him/herself with a splendid salary or profitable contracts. Or the buyer may have been trying to eliminate a competitor, regardless of the cost. In a power struggle between two factions of stockholders, shares were wanted simply because of current voting power. The buyer was completely ignorant of the company and hence the price didn't represent prevailing values or potentialities. In all of these situations, the true concept of fair market value was lacking: What a willing buyer pays to a willing seller, where each is in possession of all relevant facts and neither is under any compulsion to buy or to sell. An executor is hardly in a position to know the background of such transactions unless he/she is clued in.

Other areas where discounts in value are frequently allowed

Minority interest. If the decedent's stock in a closely-held corporation represented a minority interest, investors may be unwilling to buy it at full value. Reasons: The majority shareholders may gang up against an outsider and hence he knows that he won't be able to make his influence felt. The voting power of a minority-stock interest is usually not important. So courts generally apply discounts ranging between 15 percent and 35 percent for minority interests. Inform your executor of this situation, because otherwise he/she may fail to take it into account. You may own more shares than anyone else, but the other shareholders could be close relatives, a fact not revealed by their names. A lower value for a minority interest in real estate is also recognized as a rule.

Disposal-period discount. If property has to be sold within a stipulated time to raise money, a discount is allowable because there will be insufficient time to shop around for a proper price.

Absorption. A discount is allowed because of the price depressant caused by disposition of many parcels of land in a short period of time, creating competition among the parcels that might not otherwise exist.

Credit for tax on prior transfers

The federal estate-tax law provides for a credit for tax on prior transfers if the same property is subjected to estate tax twice (or more frequently) because two or more owners died within a 10-year period. Depending upon the time the second decedent (the one who inherited property from an earlier decedent whose estate had been taxed on this same property) held the property, the credit ranges from 20 to 80 percent. Unless you tell him/her, your executor is not likely to know that certain of your property was also included in the estate of a recently deceased relative or friend. Your estate is almost certain to forfeit this credit unless you give your executor information about property you have inherited.

Conclusions and advice

• Sell difficult-to-value property before you die so that it won't be included in your estate at a ridiculously high value in the absence of proof by the executor of a more credible figure.

• Let your executor or someone else who is trustworthy know of any value depressants that your special knowledge of the property has brought to your attention.

- Do not list property with a broker for sale at some absurdly high figure with the idea that you really don't want to sell and hence you named a figure that no one would accept. Example: Someone lists his residence for sale so that he can characterize it as a commercial property, thereby allowing him insurance and maintenance as business-expense deductions. If the individual dies, the Internal Revenue Service will predictably say that as he named the price himself, it must represent fair value.

- Do not give your executor instructions to withhold a certain property from sale. If an individual instructs or advises his executor that this property is really worth more than the market price, the IRS is likely to accept this as fact.

- Do not count on the fact that if the executor fails to reduce valuations for property because he didn't know what has been discussed in this section, he can rectify the situation by filing a refund claim based upon now-lowered valuations. If he files a refund claim, he has a tough burden of proof. And the IRS is likely to react to a refund claim by seeking something to disallow as an offset to the claim.

- There is an accuracy-related penalty, which is imposed at a rate of 20 percent, applicable to the portion of any underpayment of tax that is attributable to (1) negligence, (2) any substantial understatement of income tax, (3) any substantial valuation overstatement, and (4) any substantial overstatement of estate- or gift-tax understatement. In the case of (4), a taxpayer is subject to this penalty only if the value of any property claimed on an estate- or gift-tax return is 50 percent or less of the amount determined to be correct. The threshold below which the penalty does not apply now is $5,000. There is a 40 percent penalty in the case of valuations claimed on an estate- or gift-tax return that are 25 percent or less of the amount determined to be correct. There is a 75 percent fraud penalty, applicable to the portion of any underpayment that is attributable to fraud. (Individuals who are not familiar with the meaning of "fraud" in tax matters should discuss this with counsel.) The accuracy provisions generally apply to tax returns the due date for which (determined without regard to extensions) is after December 31, 1989.

• Before asking your spouse or a relative or friend who is financially unsophisticated in this area to serve as your executrix, trustee, or other fiduciary, consider the potential personal cost to him/her of unfamiliarity with the accuracy-related penalties, a recent provision of the law that is constantly being defined and redefined.

• The blockage rule is generally applied to stock. It also can be applied elsewhere. If an estate holds so many articles or units of a single type that individual items cannot be sold without "breaking the market," the ordinary fair market value, such as recent actual sales, can be replaced by a lower value. In a 1992 case, this was allowed where the estate owned a large number of paintings made by the decedent.

• In the case of a closely-held corporation where shares have never been sold in an arm's-length transaction, it is extremely difficult to arrive at a valuation of the stock that will be acceptable to the IRS and the courts. Have the company merge with a publicly-held or at least a better-known company when a major shareholder becomes seriously ill or simply seems to be getting on in years. The shares that you get for your original ones will now be much more susceptible to valuation. The IRS will be less arbitrary in setting a valuation if more objective factors now exist.

Chapter Thirty-nine

MINIMIZING MULTIPLE-STATE DEATH TAXES

Most states impose some form of tax upon the transfer of properties from a decedent to his/her beneficiaries. Some of these taxes are payable by the estate; others are paid by the persons who actually receive the assets. The term "death taxes" is used to cover the state taxes that are triggered by an individual's demise, regardless of whether the imposition is a property, privilege, inheritance, or succession tax. The taxes may be imposed by one state or by several states simultaneously.

Since one of the most important objectives of estate planning is to transmit as much of one's property as possible to intended beneficiaries, an individual will be thwarted in this objective if several states are able to extract death taxes from what his/her designated heirs would otherwise receive. Plans can be made, however, to minimize the danger of such multiple extractions.

Multiple state taxes upon one person's death

If an individual is subject to a state's taxing jurisdiction at the time of his death, such a tax is an accepted part of the cost of transmitting his wealth to persons of his choice. But this cost can be multiplied in the case of an individual who has lived in several states during his lifetime. Two or more states may seek to impose tax upon his property, or the receipt of it, on the ground that he was domiciled there when he died and hence is subject to the death tax.

Unfortunately, the laws of the various states define what is meant by domicile in different ways. An individual may be claimed by one state because he actually lived there at the time of his death; by another because he once lived there and that status was never terminated conclusively, even though he also lived elsewhere; by another because the decedent had property there; by another because of activities the decedent carried on there, or affiliations that he retained, or intentions that he did or did not state. The result: Two or more states may impose death taxes when an individual dies—unless he took steps to prevent this proliferation of overlapping taxes, which obviously reduces the amounts the designated beneficiaries will receive. In certain instances, such a state of affairs may even cut the beneficiaries off entirely.

The problem of the mobile executive

This potentiality is particularly serious for an executive who, during the course of his business career, is frequently transferred by his employer to new locations as promotions occur or opportunities open up. A promising individual who works for a major national corporate enterprise might well be transferred to a different locale every few years. Or a business or professional person may shift his base of operations from time to time because of changing business conditions, preferences as to where the good life is most available, or the health requirements of his family or himself. Or, when an individual retires, he may move to a more hospitable climate, taking up residence there while not exactly severing all ties to his previous place of habitation. He may at the same time have a home in each of two or more states—a residence close to his job, a winter home, a summer beachfront cottage, or a house where he expects to live when he retires.

Each of these states may claim that he was, at least in some degree, subject to its tax laws when he died. That other states may also claim him is not controlling. And under its own law, as interpreted by its own courts, each state may have a valid basis for its claim.

A mixed bag of multiple claims

One of the many spectacular examples of how a person's estate can be almost completely depleted by overlapping state death taxes was that of John T. Dorrance, head of the Campbell Soup Company. New Jersey assessed its death tax on the ground that Dorrance was domiciled in that state, paid property taxes, voted there, had church membership there, made reference to New Jersey law in his will, and died there. Pennsylvania assessed its tax on the grounds that he was born there, had a large and attractive home in the state that he occupied for a considerable length of time, and that wherever else he may have lived, his real home was there. In each instance, the highest court in the state upheld the applicability of its own death tax. The US Supreme Court refused to overturn the state courts' decisions, declaring (a) that he was domiciled in New Jersey under the law of that state when he died and (b) that he was domiciled in Pennsylvania under the law of that commonwealth when he died as well. As a result of the Court's ruling, there was very little of Dorrance's $40 million estate left for his beneficiaries, which in effect turned out to be the states of New Jersey and Pennsylvania.

Usually the problem doesn't involve real property, for one state cannot tax the transfer of property that is fixed permanently in another state. But such intangibles as securities and money, and movable property such as jewelry and works of art, may be taxed by any state whose laws cover the situation. And even though a decedent's home in State A can't be subjected to a death tax by State B, the fact that he had a home in State A does not mean that he wasn't also domiciled in State B. So multiple death taxes may be and frequently are imposed by a state in which the decedent lived for any period of time. In addition, if a decedent owned corporate stock, the state in which that company's headquarters are located may also impose death taxes.

In determining the application of one state's death taxes, it is immaterial whether the same property was also subjected to death taxes by another state. To be relieved of multiple-state death taxes, it must be shown that a wrong has been suffered through the imposition of plural taxes. That can't be established if "domicile" meets the language of two or more different states. In any event, as the Supreme Court declared in another case involving multiple-state taxes, "the Constitution of the United States does not guarantee that the decisions of state courts shall be free from error."

Change of domicile requires intent

Most frequently the problem of multiple death taxes arises after an individual has unquestionably established his domicile in a particular state. Subsequently he lives in one or more other states. The state in which he first lived, regardless of how many years ago, will still claim him unless it can be shown that his absence from the state or his residence elsewhere was coupled with an intent to terminate absolutely his domicile in that first state. For example, if someone moves to another state for reasons of health and even acquires a residence there, that doesn't mean that he won't come back to the first state when his health is better. Or he may not like his new acquaintances at the second place of abode and will return home to more congenial friends.

Presence in another state is not equated with abandonment of domicile in the first state. An instruction sheet issued by New York State declares: "A domicile once established continues until a new one is acquired. To effect a change in domicile, there must be both an intent to change domicile as well as an actual change. In deciding whether both requirements are met, a person's acts, rather than his statements, control."

In one state, a married couple with nomadic ways were deemed to be domiciled there because the couple maintained an apartment in the state, where they spent time between long sojourns at other places.

When you move, make a clean break

An individual who had served as a corporate executive in New York City and had a home in the state was deemed to be domiciled in New York at the time of her death, even though: (a) she owned a home in Florida where she spent much time, (b) declared in her will that she was a resident of Florida, and (c) paid a poll tax there. The New York court that upheld imposition of the tax pointed out that her bank accounts and safe-deposit boxes were in New York, her contributions were primarily to New York charities, and her principal social interests were in New York.

One person who had a residence in State A was deemed by the local courts to be domiciled there when he died although he was living in State B at the time of his death and voted there. The court believed that he hadn't abandoned State A as his domicile, because he continued to make use of physicians, dentists, and brokers there.

An individual who no longer lived in State A was held to be subject to its death taxes. She had valuable works of art in the state, that were insured there.

The place where one votes is not decisive, for voting requirements differ. A person who allegedly moved to State B was subject to death taxes in State A because she filed an income-tax return in that state on the resident rather than the nonresident form.

One individual owned and lived in a house in State A, which held that he was domiciled there at the time of his death. But inasmuch as he had sold this residence and was having a new one constructed for him in State B, the latter claimed him as a resident even though he had never lived in this house, on the ground that he had expressed an intent to live in State B simply by having a house built there for his own occupancy.

Maintenance of church membership in State A was held to indicate that an individual who was once domiciled there had not really severed her ties with the state even though she was living elsewhere when she died.

Conclusions and advice

• Check with local counsel as to the relevant laws of the state in which you live.

• Sever all existing ties when you move to a different state. Establish a new church affiliation, club memberships, physicians, dentists, banks, safe-deposit boxes, charities. Do not retain affiliations in a state where you once lived simply because of sentimental reasons. An individual may keep up his church affiliation in a state where he once lived because he was married there. There are less costly ways of remembering a marriage. A state can be alerted to an opportunity to assert its death tax by a newspaper item long after a former resident has moved. A typical case was a news account about someone who lived thousands of miles away from the state in which he was once domiciled. The newspaper mentioned that he "still returns to...see his doctor and dentist." Predictably, the state made a follow-up notation in its records against the time of his eventual death.

• When an individual moves from state to state, it is easy to overlook things. Check to see whether any active bank accounts have been left behind. Not only can such an account cause state-death-tax complications, but the money forgotten can be forfeited. After a number of years (which varies from state to state), an inactive bank account must be turned over to the state by a process known as escheat.

• Do not assume that because your attorney says you are now domiciled in State A, you are not also domiciled in State B for death-tax purposes. Or in States C, D, and E as well.

• File a Declaration of Domicile with the clerk of the court in the state in which you intend to reside.

Chapter Forty

USE OF LIFE INSURANCE WHILE THE INSURED IS STILL ALIVE

A rather recent development in the use of life insurance involves the obtaining by an insured person of some or all of the proceeds of insurance that is payable upon the death of the insured while he is still alive. By reason of the newness and experimental nature of such a policy, there are many variations upon this basic idea.

It may be advisable for an individual or his estate planner to shop around in order to ascertain what insurance companies recognize payments before the insured dies, what portion of the face value of the policy is available for such treatment, the premium charge for adding this feature to an existing policy, or for the purchase of a new one, what limitations if any are there on the use of the money obtained prior to death, the federal income tax treatment of amounts received, the requirement of a physical examination if a policy is modified. Variations on making use of pay-outs of the amount ordinarily payable upon the death of the insured are many. All involve use of accelerated death benefits.

Under a viatical settlement, a person with a life expectancy shortened by serious illness (defined, typically as less than two years of remaining life) agrees to accept a practical settlement for giving up his interest, say, 60 percent of the scheduled death benefit, perhaps with a cap of, assume, $500,000. The shorter the life expectancy, the greater is the agreed settlement figure, so negotiation can take place. Then the holder (now the seller) of the policy ceases making premium payments, which are made by the other party to the deal, which will collect the insurance company pay-out when death occurs. The going rate may be between 70 and 80 percent, so shop for the best percentage obtainable. Participants in an employer group plan may under a particular plan be permitted to sell their coverage. Buyers of life policies where there is a shortened life expectancy may obtain a deal by offering a finder's fee to legal or financial planners or even to physicians who have patients with very short life expectancies. Information as to parties to whom a very ill person may sell his policy may be obtained from Affording Care, a non-profit organization, at 429 East 52nd Street, Apartment 4G, New York City 10022.

Whether an insurance company charges a premium for having this benefit available depends upon the particular company. There is additional paperwork involved, so a processing fee may be charged, or perhaps the insurance company may consider this is a cost to be absorbed to be more competitive with its rivals.

In some policies, the "living benefit" may be used for any purpose.

Other plans limit the amount of money being obtained prior to death to medical expenses (where there are many interpretations) or nursing home expenses.

Sometimes the insured must be insurable when he applies for the endorsement or modification of his policy. If he now is uninsurable, he may be able to take out insurance under a substandard policy which charges a higher premium because of the greater risk being borne by the insurance company. The option to obtain accelerated benefits may not be exercisable for a specified period, such as two or three years.

Customarily, there is no recognizable policy of insurance unless the person who applies for it has an insurable interest in the life of the insured. Reason: Someone might take out an insurance policy on the life of a stranger and then arrange for a hit man to kill the insured so that the person who paid perhaps one premium could collect the face value of the policy.

An organization (viaticus) may offer to buy the regular policy of a person who needs money because he has a terminal illness or suspects that he does. This organization may buy the policy at a discount because funds are being paid out at an uncertain time prior to his life expectancy. Or the organization may be a broker who will then seek out the best available terms from companies prepared to provide high-risk coverage at an appropriate cost.

Whether this trafficking in confidential medical files that are protected by time-honored privacy is still an unsettled question.

Another still unanswered question involves the taxability of accelerated death benefits. Under most circumstances, there is no income liability except in the case of proceeds payable to a person who had bought the policy from the insured. The Internal Revenue Service regards the insurance company pay-out as proceeds of a wagering transaction, fully taxable as ordinary income. But the Service has taken the position that accelerated death benefits are not exclusions from taxable income of the insured when he dies.

If the payment of the accelerated benefit, not being a payment by reason of death, perhaps it is an annuity. The Service has not agreed with this position.

Where the person with a terminal illness had named beneficiaries covered by his policy, his ability to borrow against the policy, he will have to obtain their assent to the arrangement. If they are close and concerned relatives, of course they may do so.

A person with a terminal illness, now confronted with an unanticipated need for cash, may be able to use his insurance policy without having to sell it. He will be able to borrow against the cash surrender value of the policy, provided that this is a policy with cash surrender value (such as straight life) and that he never had surrendered incidents of ownership in the policy. A loan from the insurance company may be arranged if he had built up cash value in his policy, such as in the case of universal life. If the policy has no cash surrender value, as in the case of term insurance, he may borrow from a friend in return for naming this party to be a beneficiary of the policy. Even where a policy nominally has a cash surrender value, this already may have been used up or at least depleted by previous policy loans.

Various government aid programs are available for individuals who meet a means test. But a person who receives accelerated death benefits no longer may be eligible to meet this means test.

Chapter Forty-one

BEQUESTS IN PERCENTAGES

A will customarily makes bequests in the form of specific dollar amounts, such as, "To my beloved daughter Mabel, if she survives me, the sum of $25,000." But this standard practice makes two assumptions that may be out of line:

1. That the dollar value of the estate to be distributed is known with some reasonable degree of accuracy.

2. That there will be enough wealth available to implement the designated dollar bequests.

Dollar amount available for beneficiaries is unpredictable

Making such assumptions, especially in times of serious economic uncertainties, can be problematic. For one thing, specific dollar bequests are no guarantee that the decedent's estate will be distributed in accordance with his/her wishes—although this is the principal objective of estate planning. These factors make specific dollar bequests unadvisable:

- The actual size of an estate may depend largely on matters that can't be qualified without extensive appraisals by specialists, efforts to make arm's-length sales, or actual litigation. For example, stock in a closely-held corporation may never have been sold in a truly arm's-length transaction. In that case, how much the stock is worth is questionable. Establishment of value for federal estate-tax purposes may have to await negotiations with the Internal Revenue Service, or lawsuits that could take years. Even after a settlement is made with the IRS, the executor may have to wait some time for a buyer who will pay an acceptable price.

- Substantial assets may not be susceptible to valuation at the time a will is written. There might be unknown wealth—an inheritance, a winning lottery ticket, a long-forgotten interest in a uranium mine, an unspectacular franchise in what unexpectedly becomes a choice location, a personal injury or wrongful-death claim resulting in a large award. The very event that took the decedent's life may have made him/her wealthy.

- You may not suspect the true value of jewelry, works of art, old stock certificates, and other property. Or a nuisance-value claim might unexpectedly produce a large payout.

- Between the time of the writing of the will and the testator's death, inflation may have swollen the dollar amount of the assets mightily.

Who really benefits from dollar bequests

If the estate's assets are worth more than the testator had believed, the real beneficiary is the remainderman, who will get whatever is left after specific dollar bequests are made to the other beneficiaries. Usually, however, the remainderman is not the person for whom you would wish to provide most generously.

An individual could have the specific dollar bequests in his/her will reviewed frequently to ensure that what each beneficiary is slated to receive is realistic in the light of what the testator's wealth actually is at that time. But the certainty of a dollar bequest is just what makes it uncertain. What is the dollar itself going to be worth?

The solution: Make your bequests in the form of percentages of your estate rather than predetermined dollar amounts. Then if inflation or assets of unsuspectedly high value make the estate worth more than you had anticipated, the originally conceived allocations of your dollar worth will be self-adjusting. On the other hand, if the estate should prove to be smaller than you had anticipated, the beneficiaries you named continue to be the recipients of your bounty, but bequests will automatically be scaled down in terms of what is available at that time.

How to make percentage bequests

The percentages you apportion to the beneficiaries may be made applicable to what remains after certain specific bequests are made: a certain piece of jewelry for your sister, stock in your business for your son and daughter, dollar amounts for your favorite charities. Some specific dollar bequests could also be made to individuals, with percentages then being designated for the residue of your estate.

The percentages you select should take into account certain minimum provisions required by state law. For example, most states provide a decedent's widow with a dower or elective right to a specified percentage of her late husband's wealth that she is entitled to claim at the expense of other beneficiaries if the will has left her a lesser amount. A surviving husband may have a comparable claim, referred to as curtesy, against his wife's assets. In a few states, children are entitled to a minimum percentage of a parent's estate under specified circumstances.

Conclusions and advice

• Check with local counsel to learn the minimum percentages that the state requires you to leave in the light of dower, curtesy, and child-entitlement laws.

• Make contingency or alternative revisions of the percentages to take into account the possibility that a named beneficiary may die before you do or may renounce his/her inheritance. Consider this also in view of the fact that you and your spouse may die simultaneously.

• Do not assume that your dispositions must be on an "all or none" basis—that is, all in the form of dollar bequests or all in the form of percentages of your estate.

• Do not assume that percentage bequests will automatically make all the adjustments that are necessitated by changing circumstances. For example, this procedure will make adjustments attributed to inflation in the value of your assets. But you need to pay special attention in order to come to grips with the varying effects of inflation upon the incomes and requirements of each beneficiary. To illustrate: One beneficiary may be living on a fixed income, while another is a businessperson whose salary or profits may pretty well follow the mathematics of inflation.

Chapter Forty-two

LET GO OF ALL
RETAINED STRINGS

Now is the time to make plans so that your estate won't be unnecessarily large for tax purposes at the time of your death. This does not mean impoverishing yourself to any degree. It means letting go of the strings you may hold to various properties and interests. Perhaps there is no longer any reason for you to reserve certain courses of action that once seemed advisable. Or you may have forgotten that you possess powers over property that you don't even think of as yours.

Your estate includes property that you still control

When an individual dies, his gross estate includes the value of any property he owns. It also includes the value of property the decedent gave away many years ago, if at the time of death he still possessed any meaningful control over it. For example, if he gave away the property but retained the right to reclaim it under certain conditions, or if he had the right to say who will receive the property or its income or any part of it even though he himself can't be a beneficiary, he hasn't let go of dominion over this property. If he can control the ultimate ownership or use of assets when he dies, the actual ownership of these properties isn't determined until the moment of death—he can still control the property up to that time. So the final disposition of the assets is established only when he dies, and the value of these assets becomes part of his gross estate.

Right to change beneficiary of your insurance

There are many examples of this—some obvious, some unsuspected. Frequently an individual will take out insurance on his own life and later give the policy to another person, such as his wife. The change of ownership of the policy is recorded duly on the insurance company's books. But he reserves the right to change the name of the beneficiary, which is quite likely his spouse when he gives her the policy. Typical reason: If she should die before he does, the proceeds will go to her estate or to her nominee. And this could mean the money will go to her brother or a special friend rather than to persons the insured individual would prefer, such as his own sister. But if at the time of his death he holds any significant incident of ownership of the policy on his life, even though the policy is no longer his, the proceeds will be includable in his gross estate. These incidents include the right to change the name of the beneficiary or the power to borrow against the policy. (See Chapter Twenty-five, "Planning with Life Insurance.") Consider notifying the insurance company that you have renounced all rights you possess to modify the policy.

Retained life estate

An individual's gross estate includes the value of any property he/she has transferred that is subject to a retained life estate. For example, a husband deeds over to his wife the house in which they reside. If he continues to live there without paying rent, this will be interpreted by the Internal Revenue Service to mean that although nothing may have been said on the subject, he retained the right of occupancy until his death. So the property wasn't really hers until the moment of his death, and its value is thrown into his estate. What to do: At the time of the gift, the husband should write to his wife stating that her ownership is complete and without conditions and that he would stay in this house only if and at such times as she invited him to do so. This is not an empty gesture. In a few well-publicized situations, a wife became disenchanted with her husband, had the locks changed, and thus proved that he had indeed been living in her house only at her pleasure.

If a parent gives corporate stock to her child but reserves the right to cash the dividend checks, the value of the stock will be included in her gross estate. Her right to cash the checks, even though she does not exercise it, implies that she still owns the stock.

If an individual gives a valuable painting to a museum subject to the condition that the work of art will hang in his living room until he dies, its value will be part of his estate. Consider parting with a such art works completely.

Transfers taking effect at death

A decedent's gross estate includes the value of all transfers taking effect at his death, if until then he had the right to control or change the way in which the property was enjoyed—even though he gave the property itself away many years ago and couldn't get it back for himself despite changed wishes or economic circumstances. For example, he may have transferred money irrevocably to a trust for the benefit of his children. If he reserved the right to say how much of the trust's income or principal each child will receive each year, the trust principal will be part of his estate. On the other hand, if the trustee, a truly independent party, had full discretion as to the distribution of the income, and was familiar with and sympathetic to the grantor's desires, the same results could be obtained without estate-tax liability for the grantor. In addition, reservation of the right to apportion income might have made sense when the children were young and inexperienced and had no financial means of their own. But now they may have acquired expertise in the handling of their own money. Is it necessary to retain the strings attached to the trust funds?

Power to alter, amend, revoke, or terminate

Included in an individual's gross estate is the value of any property he had transferred in trust or otherwise in situations where, up to the moment of his death, the property was subject to his power to alter, amend, revoke, or terminate. Perhaps he never had any intention of interfering with the arrangement, but the lawyer who drew up the arrangement thought it was a good idea for his client to have flexibility. The individual should reconsider from time to time whether he needs these powers.

An individual may set up a trust for the benefit of his two children, who are identified by name. But the trust agreement allows him the right to add the names of any children who are subsequently born. So he has the right to change enjoyment of property, which would otherwise have been

268

shared only by the first two children. Should he still possess this right at the time he dies, the property is includable in his gross estate. Even if he hadn't added the name of a later-born child, he had the right to do so—and that establishes taxability. But as he grows older, the idea of more children becomes unattractive to him and his wife. Perhaps for medical reasons there can be no more children. Renunciation of the right to add additional names to the trust agreement would mean that he no longer has the right to alter or amend the existing agreements.

An individual's estate also includes the value of stock he had transferred properly to an irrevocable trust for the benefit of other persons, if he still owned 20 percent or more of the corporation's voting stock. Perhaps, as his attentions become more focused on other activities, he no longer needs to retain a 20 percent voting-stock participation in that company. He should consider whether he still wants to retain such a large interest in view of the estate-tax consequences.

Estate-tax "freeze" is narrowing

An "estate freeze" is a technique that has the effect of limiting the estate-tax value of property held by an older generation at the time of the freeze and passing any appreciation in the property to a younger generation. Generally, the older generation retains income from, or control over, the property.

In order to effect a freeze, the older generation transfers an interest in a business or other property that is likely to appreciate in value while retaining an interest in the property that is less likely to appreciate. Because the value of the transferred interest increases while the value of the retained interest remains relatively constant, the older generation has "frozen" the value of the property in the transferor's estate for estate-tax purposes.

In one common estate-freeze transaction, the "preferred interest freeze," an individual owning preferred and residual interests in a corporation or partnership transfers the residual interest to a younger generation while retaining the preferred interest. The preferred interest may enjoy preferred rights as to income or management. It may also carry discretionary rights regarding the amount, timing, or fact of payment. Such discretionary rights include: (1) a right to "put" the frozen interest for an amount equal to the liquidating preference of the frozen interest; (2) a right to liquidate an entity and to receive assets; or (3) a right to convert the nonappreciating retained interest into an appreciating interest. Another common estate-freeze transaction involves the retention of a term of years or life estate in a trust or property. For example, a parent may transfer property or money, for the ultimate benefit of a child, to an irrevocable trust in which the parent retains an income interest for a term of years. Or older and younger generations may jointly purchase them and remainder interests in property from a third party. All these transactions shift future appreciation in the property to the younger generation.

Under another common freeze device, a member of an older generation grants a member of the younger generation an option to purchase property at a fixed or formula price. Such an option may be part of a buy-sell agreement under which the survivor (or the corporation) has the right to purchase stock from the estate of the first to die. An option may freeze the value of property at the strike price, which in turn may be below the fair market value of the property at the date of death.

The transfer of a residual interest in a corporation or partnership for less than full and adequate consideration is a gift. The retention for a term of years or life estate in a trust or property is a gift if the value of the remainder interest exceeds the value of any consideration paid for such interest. Any restriction upon the sale or transfer of property, as under an option or buy-sell agreement, may reduce the fair market value for gift-tax purposes.

Prior to the enactment of the Revenue Reconciliation Act of 1990, the law provided that if an individual in effect transferred property having a disproportionately large interest of the potential appreciation in an enterprise while retaining an interest or right in the enterprise, then the transferred property was includable in his/her gross estate. Dispositions of either the transferred or retained property prior to the transferor's death resulted in a "deemed" gift equal to the amount that would have been includable had the transferor died at the time of the transfer. The law now provides that in the case of transfers made after October 8, 1990, there are new and very complicated rules designed to assure accurate determination of the value of property subject to transfer tax. The purpose: (1) to provide a well-defined and administrative set of rules; (2) to allow business owners who are not abusing the transfer tax system to engage freely in standard intrafamily transactions without being subject to severe tax consequences; and (3) to deter abuse by making unfavorable assumptions regarding certain retained rights. The taxable estate (or taxable gift) of a transferor who retained rights with possible value is increased through the assumption that the possible value is present.

The new rules, which seek to curb abuses in freezing estate-tax values through intrafamily "arrangements," also attempt to legitimize transactions that represent bona fide arrangements with extrinsically determinable valuations. The result is a complex series of provisions. Any arrangements to shift less than complete interests between family members should be discussed in advance with competent counsel.

There is no time limit for IRS assessment of gift tax in the case of an undisclosed or inadequately disclosed transfer, regardless of whether a gift-tax return was filed for other transfers in that same year. That places a strict burden of proof on disclosures to the Service of the nature of both transferred and retained rights. The taxpayer must "show his hand."

Let go!

An individual may give cash, bearer securities, or jewelry to someone else. The donor might say, "I'll keep this property for you in my safe-deposit box for reasons of security; here is a set of keys." It will take very persuasive evidence to establish that the donor hasn't retained an interest in the property if he/she also keeps a set of keys. An uncle may make a recorded gift of the funds in his savings-bank account to his niece. But if at the time of his death the money was still in this account, and he continued to have a valid signature card on file with the bank, he hadn't let go of his dominion over the property for estate-tax purposes.

Conclusions and advice

• Act promptly to sever all strings to property you no longer need. Don't retain options or powers that are not required. Cutting these strings within three years of the time you will die will not salvage the situation.

• Make a dry run through your assets with an experienced estate planner so that he/she can detect any retained strings. Let the estate planner examine the insurance policies and trust agreements, because you may not recognize traps.

- Do not assume that what made sense at the time you created ownership interests or conducted transfers still makes sense in the light of changing circumstances. Review your arrangements regularly to see whether old strings really need to be retained.

- Do not assume that you will always be more competent to make decisions than your beneficiaries, whose experience and knowledge may have removed any reason for you to continue to exercise benevolent paternalism.

- Do not continue to hold the power to say who is going to get what and when, even if you are absolutely convinced that you'll never exercise this power. It is possession of the power and not its exercise that will throw the property subject to the power into your gross estate.

- Do not think you can "freeze" the value of a business in your estate by transferring assets at this time to designated beneficiaries while retaining some control over the enterprise. Where there is a gift or other transfer to a family member and the donor (transferor) retains significant rights in the property or its income, the taxable amount of the gift includes the value of the retained right if there is genuine uncertainty as to whether the donor ever will "let go" of this interest before he/she dies. These retained rights are valued at zero for estate-tax purposes and are part of the taxable transfer. For example, powers or rights that are retained by the transferor, which are allowed to lapse, are taxed as gifts at the time of the lapse. The statute of limitations on the assessment of gift tax by the IRS does not bar assessment of the tax *at any time* if the transfer is not disclosed to the Service with sufficient detail to inform the tax people of the true nature of the transferred and of the retained interests.

Chapter Forty-three

THE DRY RUN

To avoid the many pitfalls that can frustrate the best of intentions, an individual should conduct a dry run with his/her estate planner. An excellent mechanism for this is the federal estate-tax return, Form 706. This is a formidable list of schedules, which few estate planners think of showing to their clients. But it is well worth the trouble. If the individual sees the questions and information that must be answered and supplied by somebody else after he dies, he will probably realize that he'd better supply these answers while he is still here to do so.

For example, consider "Schedule E: Jointly Owned Property." Only the owner may be in a position to show how much of the cost was furnished by other parties. Then there is "Schedule G: Transfers During Decedent's Life." There is no statute of limitations on this, and he is probably the only one who knows of such transfers and can supply full details.

Other schedules, when brought to the testator's attention, can be used to obtain information he probably didn't even know was necessary. Some schedules may involve matters he never really understood, such as "Schedule H: Powers of Appointment." "Schedule D: Insurance on Decedent's Life" can be used to ascertain whether he has retained any incident of ownership, such as the right to change the name of the beneficiary or to borrow against the policy. "Schedule M: Bequests, etc., to Surviving Spouse" can be used to distinguish between deductible and nondeductible interests, with the opportunity of providing for qualified terminable interest property or eliminating terminable interests if that is now desired. Now may be the time to explore ways in which the marital deduction can best be utilized, and if that really is desirable under present circumstances. For married couples, provision can be made for full utilization of the unified credit in both estates.

There is "Schedule Q: Credit for Tax on Prior Transfers." The testator is probably the only person who can establish his estate's entitlement to this credit. This refers to property that was inherited from anyone whose death preceded his by less than 10 years, assuming that that person's estate was subject to tax.

"Schedule O: Charitable, Public, and Similar Gifts and Bequests" should lead to inquiry into whether the donees are still on an all-important, ever-changing IRS-approved list. Ascertain, preferably by an affirmative statement from the major donees involved, that discrimination is not being practiced. Was anything promised to you, perhaps by unilateral action, by a recipient or designated donee? If so, decline it in writing.

The federal estate-tax form calls for information about the decedent's personal representative, which should focus attention on who the executors are. Are such persons still qualified, interested, and willing to do the job competently? Are successors or contingent executors named? A certified copy of the will is called for. Who knows where the latest version of this document is located? Has it been reviewed in the light of family and economic changes, or modifications in the law? Is the will where it can be obtained instantly upon the death of the decedent? If the will is in his/her safe-deposit box, remember that this is probably going to be sealed by the bank until it can be opened in the presence of a representative of the state tax commission or the Internal Revenue Service. That delay may not be desirable.

Information is asked about any individual who receives benefits from the estate, "for example, as beneficiary of a trust...." This should be the basis for investigating any retained rights the testator had in the trust, such as the right to change dispositions or modify any arrangement. The advisability of severing any retained interests should be reviewed. The actual trust instrument should be examined, for an individual's recollection of it can prove unsatisfactory.

Conclusions and advice

• Even if your will, insurance policies, trust agreements, and other documents were prepared by persons highly competent in those areas, have them checked by somebody who has estate-planning expertise. An individual who is highly knowledgeable in wills, for example, may be uninformed about current tax legislation and the special language of the estate- or other tax laws. For example, a specialist in wills may not appreciate the tax significance of a general power of appointment that is not referred to as such, or a reverse-simultaneous-death clause.

• See that your attorney, accountant, and executor carry ample malpractice insurance.

• Do not rely on answers or advice from the Internal Revenue Service. This advice may not be correct, or your questions to the IRS may not have been complete. See *Your Rights as a Taxpayer*, IRS Publication 1.

• Do not assume that your attorney, accountant, and executor have up-to-date familiarity with estate planning. This is a highly technical specialty with which a generalist may not be at home.

• Make certain that your executor-to-be sees a blank federal estate-tax return so that he/she will know what has to be prepared, or supervised, or at least signed. Would this person have doubts as to what he/she is getting into? Will he/she refuse to serve, which might make it necessary for a court to name a replacement?

• The dry run should include the recognition of areas on the tax return that may be probed by the IRS. For example, there are increasingly severe accuracy-related and other penalties. Attach to your tax return Form 8275, "Disclosure Statement." This form (assuming that it is properly prepared) advises the Service of items or positions that you take which you are able to document. Then, even if ultimately it is determined that your position was incorrect, you are not subjected to the accuracy-related penalty by reason of negligence or disregard of the rules. Use Form 8275R, "Regulation Disclosure Statement," for disclosures of positions contrary to IRS regulations.

Chapter Forty-four

A LETTER TO YOUR EXECUTOR

Few people take enough trouble to make a comprehensive plan to pass as much property to designated beneficiaries as is humanly possible by taking steps to avoid erosion of the estate. What is involved here is undramatic but effective: providing any kind of information or records that will be needed by your executors to maximize the estate. This also means taking precautions against the diminution of the estate due to inadequate records.

Justifying your income-tax returns

For example, the correctness of federal income-tax returns can probably be established to a considerable degree when audited. The taxpayer may be able to explain why certain items weren't shown as taxable income, because they were inheritances, gifts, or repayments of loans he made. He should be in a position to show how much he paid in past years for securities recently sold, or the nature of items claimed as medical expenses. He may be able to demonstrate the original cost of jointly-owned property that was furnished by one or more co-owners. If these tax returns are examined by the Internal Revenue Service when the taxpayer is no longer here to explain or document his handling of various items, tax will predictably be increased by default. Such unnecessary tax deficiencies, accompanied by penalties and interest, reduce the amount of what is available to the beneficiaries.

Does anybody else know where your tax records, workpapers, and backup information and documents are located? Is there anyone who can explain to a suspicious revenue agent what you have done and why? The burden of proof is on the taxpayer—even though deceased.

Defense against claims

Far more information may be required for other purposes than taxation. Claims of every conceivable nature could be filed against the decedent's estate; will anyone be able to prove from checkbooks or corre-spondence whether these amounts have been paid or settled? Somebody may insist that he/she actually owns real estate, jewelry, or other items that were in the decedent's possession at the time of death. Does anyone else know the location of deeds, titles, bills of sale, invoices, receipts? When property is destroyed or stolen, is there any insurance covering it? Who are the insurers, and where are the policies and endorsements?

An individual may have relied heavily on his accountant, lawyer, broker, or insurance agent to provide answers about his/her affairs. Does anybody know who these people are or were? Even the decedent's accountant may not know who prepared the tax returns two years ago and who has the workpapers that could provide the IRS with acceptable answers.

An individual may have anticipated that information about his affairs would be needed after his death. But he should ensure that his efforts to provide it are not thwarted by someone else's unawareness of the practical problems involved. Specifically, he should leave unmistakable instructions with his spouse, children, housekeeper, or other party who is in a position to "clean up the house" that nothing is to be thrown away in the event of his death until the matter has been discussed with his accountant, attorney, or executor.

Briefing your executor

Your designated executor must be in a position to represent you after your death. To do so, he/she has to be in possession of all facts, figures, and substantiation that you would have at your disposal were you required to make explanations, to prove them, and to take action. Your executor can only do his/her best for you, your estate, and your beneficiaries if you clue him in fully on what he/she must know.

What to tell your executor

You should write a letter to him/her at this time, letting him/her know all about your belongings, records, and financial affairs. Update this letter periodically with postscripts and corrections as needed. If you don't want to reveal anything at this time, seal the envelope, but leave it where it can be found—by attaching it to your will, for example. The following items should be mentioned in this extremely important letter:

1. The location of the final executed version of your will.

2. The location of your cemetery plot and its deed or registration certificate. These should not be in your safe-deposit box, because they may be required at once, and a bank will probably deny access to your box until it can be opened in the presence of a tax officer. Are there any specific instructions about burial for your executor?

3. Names and addresses of the designated guardians for your minor children should they be orphaned by your death, or by the simultaneous deaths of both you and your spouse.

4. The location and identifying number of your safe-deposit box. Where are the keys, or what is the lock combination? Does anyone else have access to this box? If so, the executor should be asked to take inventory before anybody can take other things.

5. The location of all checking and savings-bank accounts, with identifying account numbers. Who has the power of attorney or signature authorization to draw on these accounts? Should a stop be placed on withdrawals?

6. Credit-card accounts and numbers. Your executor should cancel these at once to prevent unauthorized charges to your accounts. Even if you carry credit-card insurance, such charges create time-consuming problems and uncertainty.

7. What was the source of any cash in a safe-deposit box or in your home or office? In the absence of proof to the contrary, the Internal Revenue Service will consider any unexplained cash to represent previously untaxed

income. This presumption can be refuted if there is credible evidence. For example, there may be a letter to your executor stating that Social Security checks or horse track winnings (reported) will be converted into cash, to be kept in the box as an emergency fund. Correspondence can identify cash as having been found money, which was turned over to the police department and given back to the finder when no claimant appeared.

8. Location of any bank accounts that are not in your name. Example: Deposits in a numbered bank account in Switzerland. Many Swiss bank accounts have been lost because no one except the decedent knew the number. Secrecy can be carried too far.

9. The location and description of any property that is not certain to come to the attention of the executor. You may have lent your daughter-in-law jewelry for an indefinite period. You may have sent property on consignment to a dealer to be sold when a specified price could be obtained. Property may have been deposited as collateral for a loan.

10. The best market for properties that you own. Someone may have expressed interest in purchasing your house, which is next door to his. You may have unusual belongings of some nature that can best be sold in special markets or to hobbyists or collectors unlikely to be known to your executor, even if he/she is a thorough professional.

11. What are the names and addresses of your accountant, attorney, insurance agent, bank officer, realtor? Who is your physician? The executor may have to prove that you were mentally competent at the time you wrote your will, set up a trust agreement, or accepted or transferred property.

12. Schedule of life insurance owned, with identifying policy numbers. Location of the policies themselves. Remember to include employer group-

insurance certificates where the employer has the master policy. Include policies that have lapsed; they may still have some value.

13. Schedule of property, liability, malpractice, umbrella, and other insurance. This may provide the means of obtaining reimbursement, show the location and description of property, and save the estate from the consequences of a lawsuit.

14. Brokers' confirmation slips for all purchases of securities. This will establish the original cost of all securities sold. If these slips have already been discarded, note the dates shown by transfer agents on stock certificates and registered bonds. This at least provides some indication of the time of purchase, and prices at that time can be established from newspaper files or from reference books. Keep all letters from corporations or their financial representatives about stock dividends, split-ups, rights, and reorganizations. These may modify the figure, your tax basis, by establishing what you originally paid for the securities.

15. List of names and addresses of all prior employers, regardless of when your employment by them terminated. Many corporate pension plans provide vested rights after certain periods of service, to be payable at some designated future time (such as your 65th birthday) or upon the occurrence of a stated event, even though you are no longer with the company.

16. If you work for a corporation that is subject to the Pension Reform Act of 1974 (in general, any company engaged in interstate commerce), the employer is required by law to provide you with a complete description of its pension plan. You must also be provided with various computations of your rights under the plan. Keep these, for they may well provide explanations of entitlements that should be claimed when you

reach a certain age or die.

17. Record of any governmental employment at any time, such as in the armed forces. Show the branch of service, your serial number, and the approximate periods involved. There may be some form of forgotten or misunderstood veterans' or survivors' rights.

18. Copies of income-tax returns without regard to the dates of statutes of limitations. Don't discard these after three years or any other date. Sometimes the statute of limitations doesn't apply to a particular tax return, such as where there was some omission that caused the submission to be characterized as "no return." Also, the returns may contain useful information.

19. Location of current and past checkbooks and canceled checks. These could furnish proof that bills and claims have been paid. This material can also indicate the cost of particular property, information that is essential in the case of casualty losses or establishment of the tax basis of property.

20. Location of birth certificate. This can be important for such purposes as pensions, Social Security primary and derivative rights, and company retirement programs. If you don't have a birth certificate, leave a record of your date and place of birth. A passport, even an expired one, may be useful here.

21. Location of marriage certificate. This may be useful for such purposes as the marital deduction, joint gifts, determination of dower and curtesy rights, and survivors' rights.

22. Divorce decree or reference to the court that issued it, with the

date. This is essential in the case of the marital deduction, where there may be a question as to who is the decedent's surviving spouse.

23. What federal gift-tax returns have you filed at any time? When and where were they filed? What names appeared on them? Where are your copies of the returns?

24. The names and dates of death of any persons from whom you have inherited property. With this information, an executor may be able to claim a credit for the tax on prior transfers if the person from whom you inherited property died within 10 years of your demise. State the name of that person's executor if you know it. You probably received correspondence from him/her, or a release form to sign. Preserve these.

25. Have you been named in connection with reversionary, contingent, or remainder rights in a will or trust agreement, yours or someone else's? There may be potential interests to be investigated by your executor, provided you furnish a lead.

26. If you ever set up a trust, regardless of when, specify where a copy of the trust agreement is located. There may be rights to be claimed.

27. Have you ever guaranteed or endorsed a note or somebody else's obligation? Your executor may be able to settle any claims before they mature.

28. Does anyone owe you money? Have you lent out property? Advise your executor as to what documentation or proof there is. Were there any witnesses, any correspondence?

29. Are there any pending tax or other refund claims? Should there be?

30. Are there any unfavorable factors that could justify your execu-

tor's valuing any of your property at less than fair market value? (See Chapter Thirty-eight, "Valuations of Estate Assets.")

31. Have you any affirmative statements from approved charitable organizations to which you made contributions or bequests that they are not engaging in any form of discrimination? (See Chapter Thirty-five, "Avoiding Disallowance of Charitable Bequests.")

32. Have you received any income in respect of a decedent? This is income earned by but not yet taxed to someone from whom you have received an inheritance. The value of this person's right to receive the income was included in the estate tax paid for him/her. The beneficiary is entitled to deduct a portion of the estate tax, based upon the ratio of the right's value to the decedent's total assets.

You might advise your executor on which lawyers, accountants, appraisers, or other specialists to engage; but this should be only a recommendation.

Conclusions and advice

• If you move to a different state, have a new will prepared by a lawyer who practices there. The will should be signed by resident witnesses.

• You or your adviser should be aware of how long various types of documents should be retained. Obtain from the Government Printing Office a copy of *Guide to Federal Records Retention Requirements.*

• Advise your spouse or other persons concerned not to be too hasty in throwing away your papers and files. There could be great temptation to throw things away if the family moves to smaller quarters after your death. Such destruction greatly complicates the work of an executor, increasing his/her fee and reducing the amount available to beneficiaries.

• Churn inactive bank accounts so that the monies will not go to the state where the deposit was located on the ground that no one claimed ownership within the period specified by state law.

• Do not allow anyone other than an attorney skilled in estate planning to draw up your will, trust agreement, or other document. At least have someone who is knowledgeable in this specialized field review your regular attorney's draft in order to make certain that the particular requirements for the marital deduction, powers of appointment, and the like are taken into account.

• Do not assume that your estate's assets can be readily recognized and collected by your fiduciary. Leave a paper trail for your executor to follow.

• If your designated executor is not familiar with serving in this capacity, advise him/her not to sell any of your property before paying the federal estate tax. Recently it was held that a hasty executor was personally liable for the tax when insufficient estate assets remained to pay this tax.

• Help your executor to avoid penalties for undervaluation of property values, as discussed on page 246. Endeavor to provide him/her with all relevant facts.

• Urge him to make a conscientious effort to estimate what the estate tax will be. Otherwise the estate may not have enough cash or readily realizable assets to pay the estate tax within the required nine months. In that case, valuable assets may have to be jettisoned at the wrong time.

Chapter Forty-five

MAINTENANCE OF CONFIDENTIALITY

The customary manner of distributing property at the time of one's death is the will. But a will must be regarded as public information, for when it is submitted to the appropriate local court for approval (probate), the document is placed on file, where it may be examined by interested parties or by the merely curious or inquisitive. An individual may not wish to have the public at large know what he/she is leaving to certain persons or who has been cut out of the will. With some advance planning, it is possible to keep this information confidential.

Trust agreements aren't public documents

Although wills are "published"—that is, made available to the public—trust instruments are not. So one of the advantages of using a trust is the confidentiality of transfers. A will can set up a testamentary trust, with

288

designated property passing to the trustees. The person for whose benefit the trust was set up, allocation of the properties to various parties, details as to the interests of life tenants and remaindermen, and the like are known only to the decedent, the trustees, and the local court if it is called upon by the interested parties to decide whether a trustee has lived up to his/her fiduciary responsibilities. The Internal Revenue Service is also entitled to examine trust instruments, but by law the Service and its agents are forbidden to make any revelations to outsiders. As a result, the public is excluded from knowledge about the contents of trust instruments.

Compare this to dispositions by will. For example, in 1976 a superior court judge in New Jersey refused to permanently seal the will of William Randolph Hearst on the ground that this would be equivalent to denying the public the right to know what was done in the probate court.

An inter vivos trust (see Chapter Three, "The Trust as Financial Umbrella") achieves confidentiality in the making of transfers during a donor's lifetime; no one has access to details of property dispositions after they have been made to the trust.

Co-ownership of property as a form of will

An individual may use a form of property ownership that takes the place of a will in disposing of assets at the time of his/her death. (See Chapter Eighteen, "Choice of Forms of Ownership.") If he/she owns property jointly with someone else, with rights of survivorship in each co-owner, the property automatically passes to the surviving co-owner(s) upon the demise of one co-owner. No outsider needs to know of this co-ownership with right of survivorship clauses. Unpublicized passage of this property to the survivor isn't affected by the fact that the IRS includes the full value of the jointly-held property in the gross estate of the first co-owner to die in the absence of sufficient proof by the estate's executor that part of the property actually was owned by someone else. The value of the entire property may be included in the decedent's estate for tax purposes, but the property itself passes to the survivor(s). It is not subject to probate, with its publicity and delays, for the executor has nothing to administer and nothing to account for. The property isn't the decedent's after he/she dies. Everything has been arranged for prior to the appointment of the executor.

Joint accounts

Joint bank accounts or joint brokerage accounts may be established with an intended beneficiary. The latter becomes the sole owner upon the death of the person who created the account if it is set up in the proper fashion. If the party who is named co-owner of the account makes no contribution to it, or withdrawal from it, setting up the account creates no federal gift-tax liability for the individual who funds the account. Only the bank or broker knows about what happens.

Disposition by gift

Property can avoid the necessity of disposition by a published will if it is given away during the owner's lifetime. As a rule, the very persons who would receive the property at the time of the decedent's death would be the natural objects of his bounty in the case of gifts given during his lifetime as well.

Avoidance of litigation

Regardless of how an individual makes disposition of his/her estate at or prior to death, details may become available to the public if there is litigation involving the estate, the will, or earlier dispositions that reduced the size of the estate. What happens during a court trial is customarily published in printed transcripts of the hearing. Any curious or interested party can read these printed reports. For example, if a tax question is involved, the judge's decision, generally preceded by a detailed account of the facts and figures, is published in loose-leaf tax services that are available to many attorneys, accountants, and libraries by subscription. If the question is interesting or important enough, financial publications or even the local press will pick up the story from there.

To avoid this publicity, an individual may make plans to minimize the possibility of litigation. Lawsuits might arise from either of two principal sources:

1. The IRS may force litigation if agreement on tax differences can't be reached, for example, in the valuation of stock in a closely-held corporation. Seek to make a compromise with the Service to avoid litigation, which is usually costly and unpredictable. Consider yielding entirely in the dispute if there seems to be an irreconcilable difference of opinion to avoid the risk of publicity that could result from court action and publication of the details.

2. Disappointed heirs may challenge the will in court, perhaps on the ground that undue influence was exerted upon the decedent or that he/she was mentally unsound at the time the will was signed. This, too, might be settled by the executor and the other heirs before the matter actually goes

to trial with its resultant publicity. Alternatively, some individuals make provisions in their wills providing that if any beneficiary contests in court what he is designated to receive or the validity of the will as a whole, his bequest is to be canceled automatically in favor of another named party, the remainderman, or a designated charitable organization.

Conclusions and advice

• Work out in advance with your beneficiaries what jewelry, real estate, securities, etc., each one will receive so that squabbles can be ironed out before the will is finalized.

• Leave percentages to your beneficiaries in your will so that no description of property or identification of a dollar amount is available to the public.

• Do not assume that your executor will be discreet.

• Do not assume that dispositions in your will are of no interest to anyone except individuals designated as beneficiaries.

• Do not rely on joint ownership of property to eliminate the need for a will. Jointly-owned property with right of survivorship can be substituted for a will, but presumably you will also have other property that isn't co-owned, perhaps for good reason. If you don't have a will, this property will be distributed according to the state's intestacy laws.

• Any confidential information that could produce additional tax if "leaked" to the IRS by someone familiar with the facts could be "squealed" to the Service in return for a share in taxes that are collected as a result of this information. In addition, the informant's identity is protected by law.

Chapter Forty-six

AVOIDING APPOINTMENT OF AN ADMINISTRATOR

One of an individual's greatest responsibilities to his/her estate and beneficiaries is to make realistic plans for the selection of the proper executor or executrix. But the person or persons painstakingly selected may not actually serve in this capacity. They may have died, lost interest, or become incompetent, or they may simply be "unavailable" when the time arrives. Another possible problem is that the decedent's will can't be accepted for administration (probate) because of technical shortcomings, such as lack of the minimum number of witnesses stipulated by state law.

In either of these cases, the local court that has jurisdiction over decedents' estates will name an administrator or administratrix. Such a person would have powers similar to those of the nonexistent or nonqualified executors.

Shortcomings of administrators

A court-appointed administrator is unlikely to have any concern for your beneficiaries and their interests. He may not have the knowledge or ability to implement your plans. He may be a relative of the judge—or even a political crony with no interest in the administration of your estate beyond collecting his fee, which he is unlikely to try to keep as low as possible. It is not even required that he be competent.

Obviously, not all administrators fall into this dismal classification. The administrator may be even more suitable than the person you named. But you can't afford to take a chance on what sort of administrator will be named if you have failed to make proper plans to ensure that someone of your choice, who feels a sense of responsibility to you because you selected him/her, will serve. It is, most assuredly, in the best interest of your estate plan and your beneficiaries that you do so.

How an administrator can be counterproductive

An administrator's performance can hurt your estate in the following ways:

1. He/she may fail to collect all of the estate's assets by neglecting to make a diligent and careful search for property of every kind left by the decedent. The discovery and gathering in of the decedent's properties may require a great deal of hard work and imagination.

2. The estate may be subjected to unnecessary penalties and interest payments because of sloppy or tardy filing of the estate-tax and other returns. In some instances, the beneficiaries can compel an administrator to bear the consequences of his mistakes out of his own pocket. But few

beneficiaries know this.

3. Amounts may be paid out to otherwise valid claimants whose rights are unenforceable under state law because of late submission or technical reasons.

4. The administrator may devote too little time and vision to the task of seeking out the best markets for estate assets that must be sold to raise funds.

5. Indifference may be displayed to the pleas of beneficiaries for prompt honoring of bequests. This may at least in part be the result of the administrator's inexperience in this sort of thing; that is, he/she may be so fearful of making a mistake that could penalize him personally that he pays out nothing to beneficiaries until the estate is wound up and the federal tax liability is finally determined. That could take years. For example, if an executor or administrator has any knowledge that the distribution of estate assets would jeopardize the ability of the Internal Revenue Service to collect its taxes, or reason to believe that this may be so, he can be held personally responsible for distributions that leave the IRS without payment. This rule does not apply, however, if the administrator has no reason to believe that the IRS has claims that would be imperiled by his implementing a bequest made in the will.

6. To avoid difficult or time-consuming problems, the administrator may dump estate assets too quickly to obtain the best possible price. For example, he may wish to wash his hands of the work involved in running the decedent's business, which could be a very important estate asset. In consequence, the business may be liquidated or otherwise disposed of in excessive, expensive haste. Actually, the decedent may have wished to

have the business continued so that in time his/her children could take over the operation. The administrator here, instead of seeking to implement the decedent's objectives, has frustrated them.

7. The estate may be kept open too long so that the administrator can "earn" more fees, and these fees will come out of the pockets of those who may have a better right to the money.

8. Insurance may not have been obtained on estate-owned assets. Perhaps the type of insurance required couldn't have been obtained without extensive shopping around.

9. The administrator may not be honest. This could also be the case with an executor, of course. But presumably the testator took great care to select someone whose probity was substantially demonstrated many times.

How to avoid the naming of an administrator

To ensure that an executor of your selection will serve, this is what you should do:

1. Sound out your designated executor to see whether he/she will actually serve if named in your will. Do this periodically. Is this person's health still satisfactory? Has he taken on full-time responsibilities elsewhere? Is he still interested in you and your beneficiaries? If not, replace him.

2. Seek to ensure your designated executor's agreement to serve by recommending knowledgeable and able attorneys, accountants, and (where appropriate) appraisers and brokers who can help him carry out his responsibilities without excessive detail work with which he isn't familiar.

3. Name one or more successor or contingent executors so that if the

person of your choice doesn't serve, at least it will be your second or third choice rather than an administrator whom you would never have engaged.

4. Name a trust company as co-executor. This virtually assures the permanence and continuity of an executor you have seen fit to name.

5. Make certain that your will is valid so that the executor chosen by you will qualify. Have an attorney who is familiar with state law check such requirements as the minimum number of witnesses necessary. State laws vary on the technicalities to be met.

6. Be sure that your will can be found when the time comes to have it probated. A perfectly executed and technically correct will is useless if nobody knows where it is. Leave your will in your attorney's office, or with your federal income-tax work papers.

Conclusions and advice

• Make available to your executor-to-be the names of your attorney, accountant, broker, insurance agent, and other persons knowledgeable in aspects of your affairs so that the best job possible can be done. Otherwise the executor you have named may be removed by the court as incompetent, to be replaced by an administrator. (See Chapter Forty-four, "A Letter to Your Executor.")

• Make plans to keep your business out of the hands of an administrator. (See Chapter Twenty-four, "Business-Continuation Arrangements.")

• Advise your attorney, spouse, or any other person who is interested in your affairs to take action if for any reason your named executor isn't able to serve. For example, if the will is technically flawed and therefore inadmissible to probate, have the court petitioned to name as administrators the individuals you have chosen as executors. (Unfortunately, you can't be sure the court will agree.)

• Do not assume that the executors named in your will are going to outlive you, or will be perpetually willing to serve, or will preserve their present competences indefinitely.

• Do not name as executor or executrix a spouse, an adult child, or a friend whose inexperience is apt to result in performance so poor that a court will replace him/her with an administrator.

• Choose as executor a person who will not resign in frustration after he discovers that certain information he must use simply is not available to an unimaginative, routine party. Actually, a resourceful person may be able to discover whether there are any insurance policies on the decedent's life although the policies themselves or even premium notices cannot be found. He could call the National Consumers Insurance Helpline, which operates a missing policy service—1-800-942-4242. Ask for missing policy questionnaire. The name, address, etc., of the decedent then is forwarded by this group to all companies that participate in the Helpline (unfortunately, all insurers are not participants in the program). Any company which had issued a policy will then communicate with the executor. Heirs or other persons who may know where the decedent had assets may be traced. A live-wire executor could consult Joseph J. Culligan, *You Too Can Find Anybody: A Reference Manual.* Order from the author at 499 5 NW 79 Avenue, Miami, Florida 33166.

Chapter Forty-seven

THE TAX ADVANTAGES OF LIFE ABROAD

As you approach retirement, you may want to consider giving up residence in the United States, and even renouncing your US citizenship. There are substantial estate- and gift-tax savings to be had when the proper steps are taken. Indeed, these taxes may not only be reduced but entirely eliminated. That obviously means a greater amount of assets for your beneficiaries.

Anyone contemplating becoming a nonresident alien in order to take advantage of the tax benefits, however, must be very careful. If the Internal Revenue Service thinks that you are becoming an expatriate and renouncing citizenship principally for tax-avoidance purposes, you may have acted in vain if you die within 10 years of giving up your citizenship. As a corollary, the sooner you implement your decision to become a nonresident alien, the better.

A trail of documents

To forestall adverse IRS action, you must lay the groundwork for your new life outside of the United States with contemporaneous documentary evidence of your reasons for adopting expatriate status in the first place, such as:

Health. As an individual gets older, his/her physical well-being may require an environment that is not readily available in the United States.

Proximity to family. One's spouse, friends, and acquaintances may be dead, and the company of adult children who have established residence abroad for business or other reasons may be desirable.

Finances. Life abroad can be cheaper, a significant factor that may have to be taken into account when salary or business income ceases.

The good life. Residence in Europe will make it possible to frequent the continent's great cultural centers on a continuing basis. The retiree may wish to return to his/her family roots when closer relatives are no longer alive.

Contemporaneous evidence, such as medical reports and recommendations, lawyers' opinions, bills of sale, letters from friends describing their new life abroad, or invitations to move into the homes of adult children now permanently established in a foreign land must be convincing enough to meet the burden of proof that will confront the executor of your estate if the IRS challenges your motives for giving up citizenship.

And, of course, if you are going to reside in a foreign country, there are many reasons for giving up US citizenship, including:

1. A conscience-free way to devote all of your loyalties to your adopted homeland.

300

2. A practical means of canceling the disadvantages of US citizenship for the full-time resident of another country. Examples: in certain countries, the rights of a foreigner (a US citizen, in this situation) to hold real estate there; engaging in an activity where licensing is required and questionnaires must be completed.

Good news for taxpayers with nonresident alien status . . .

For a noncitizen living abroad, the federal tax advantages are considerable:

Gross estate, for federal tax purposes, means only property located in the United States at the time of death. The gross estate of a US citizen or resident includes all of his/her property, wherever it is located.

There is no federal gift tax on the transfer of intangible property, such as stocks.

There is no federal income tax on income earned abroad.

. . . And the bad news

Offsetting these benefits, however, are some problems:

If a nonresident alien, such as a bona fide expatriate, owns property in the United States at the time of his death, it will be includable in his gross estate. To discourage an expatriate from transferring such property to a foreign corporation (one with a charter that wasn't issued by one of the 50 states) in exchange for its stock so that he won't own property here at the time of his death, the tax law provides that his gross estate here will include the same proportion of the value of his stock in the foreign corporation that its property in this country bears to its total property. The rule applies where the deceased person had owned 10 percent or more of the foreign corporation's voting stock when he died, or if he and certain close relatives together owned more than 50 percent of the combined voting power. He is also deemed to own stock in a foreign corporation under general provisions of the federal estate-tax law if he transferred the stock to a trust in which he had retained significant powers.

If citizenship was renounced within 10 years of his death, a nonresident alien's estate will be taxed as though he were still a citizen at the moment of his death "unless such loss [of citizenship] did not have as one of its principal purposes the avoidance of taxes...."

Transfers of intangible property by nonresident aliens are not exempt from federal gift tax if the donor gave up his citizenship within the same 10-year period subject to the same condition.

Ordinarily, the burden of proof is on the taxpayer. But here the IRS must establish that it is reasonable to believe that the expatriate's loss of US citizenship would, were it not for this provision, result in a substantial reduction in the estate, inheritance, legacy, and succession taxes. If this is established, then the executor bears the burden of proving that the loss of citizenship did not have as one of its principal purposes the avoidance of federal income, estate, or gift taxes. If renunciation takes place more than 10 years before death, however, there is no such presumption to be refuted.

Since no one can forecast his own demise, renunciation of citizenship should follow swiftly after any decision to give up living in the United States.

Exception to the 10-year rule

The tax law exempts two classes of nonresident aliens from the 10-year rule:

1. Those whose loss of citizenship resulted from deportation proceedings instituted under the Immigration and Naturalization Act.

2. Those who had acquired dual citizenship at birth and lost US citizenship by residing for a specified period in the foreign country of their choice. Example: Someone born in a foreign country (where the law provides for dual citizenship under certain circumstances) of an American mother, whose nationality furnished him/her with US citizenship. Remember that laws and treaties involving foreign countries are not consistent. Check with an attorney who is familiar with the statutes of the country involved. Or get in touch with that country's consulate in the United States.

Conclusions and advice

• Anticipate that the IRS will question your bona fide intentions as a nonresident alien. You will not be around to explain the nontax reasons for your renunciation of citizenship; that task will be your executor's. So provide him/her with the necessary documentation.

• Questions involving acquisition of citizenship abroad should be referred to attorneys who specialize in the laws of the particular country involved. You may find that the country in which you are interested has a consulate in this country where information may be obtained.

• Do not delay renunciation of US citizenship if that is your intention. Death within 10 years of that act can thwart your intentions.

• Modern technology now gives individuals the opportunity to live wherever they choose, regardless of where their work is performed. Computers, fax machines, modems, 2-way interactive video teleconferencing make it possible so that there is no geographical relationship between where you live and where your work is performed. An individual or a corporate enterprise can hire experts and technicians in any part of the world, who can send the products of their assignments anywhere electronically.

- Large numbers of US citizens, especially wealthy ones, are leaving this country to avoid confiscatory taxes (existing and threatened). There are widespread rumors that an exit tax would be imposed on persons leaving the country, such as an additional capital gains tax on unsold assets. Transfer of assets to foreign trusts could be covered.

- There is a $70,000 annual tax exemption for foreign-source income earned by US citizens residing abroad; but this exemption does not apply to investment income. This might encourage citizens residing abroad to renounce their present citizenship.

- *International Living* is a publication designed to show where to live abroad to obtain the best advantages as well as tax other benefits. Write to 105 West Monument Street, PO Box 17473, Baltimore, MD 21298.

- Advertisements in magazines that are read throughout the world (such as *The Economist*) frequently tell how easy it is to obtain a second passport, with obvious advantages in disclosure of address and residency.

Index